Dear FUTURE WIFE®

A Man's Guide and a Woman's Reference to
Healthy Relationships

BASHEA WILLIAMS

ELOHAI
INTERNATIONAL
PUBLISHING & MEDIA

Published by ELOHAI International Publishing & Media

P.O. Box 64402
Virginia Beach, VA 23467
Elohailntl.com

Cover Design by ELOHAI International Publishing & Media

Library of Congress Control Number: 2018963018

ISBN: 978-1-7358639-0-0

Printed in the United States of America

Dear FUTURE READER,

To my brother reading this:

It's time to decide.

You say you want an independent woman but can't handle her "no." You say she's not listening, but you haven't learned how to speak. You say you're fearless, but you're afraid to be vulnerable with her. You say you want a classy lady, but your search engine reveals lust. You say you're the head, but you struggle with making the right decisions for your own life. You say you want your family back, but you continue to put what it takes for that to happen on the back burner. You ask for forgiveness and each time you do the same thing you wouldn't tolerate. You say you want someone who is down, but have yet to master helping her up. You say you don't like the "modern women," but you still operate in your old ways. You say she's insecure, but you utilize that to defend actions that instill and promote insecurity.

You struggle with communicating your feelings because you haven't been taught and really don't want to learn how. This—today— is the perfect time to learn. You want her to pray for you while you prey on her. You tell or ask yourself, "She has everything she needs, so what can I really give her?" instead of valuing *you* as the missing piece (her peace). You're confusing "protecting" yourself with hurting her. You know how to put your mind, body, and soul into everything except her and the relationship (refer back to the third sentence).

To my sister reading this:

It's time to decide.

You say you want a strong man, but are annoyed with his strength, so you call him stubborn. You want God's best but haven't given God your best. You say you want a man to take care of you, but you haven't defined what that means for you as opposed to comparing what other men do for other women. Or, you want him to take care of you like you take care of yourself. (Remember: he has not had the chance to get to know you like you know you.) You handle him like a business deal, because you have learned to master corporate America. You're a "boss," but have a hard time with love because you can't control it. You want him to share, and yet what's yours is yours because you've earned it. You mentally and emotionally designed a "real relationship" before considering a real relationship with a real person. You say you don't want to date anyone like your "ex," but you focus on your ex's traits in him. You want someone to treat you differently, but you continue to choose the same things, present yourself the same way, and attract the same energy.

We must ask ourselves what do we really want, need, and are able to accept. There is always a compromise. There will always be imperfections, but relationships aren't about finding someone who will do what we want; they are about accepting what the person we want can give. This isn't to say that you accept any and every person with their flaws. I write that to remind you to ask yourself a key question about your potential or current significant other, "If this person were to remain the same, could I remain in the relationship?" Then decide!

Dear Future Wife is going to present you with many decisions and deciding moments. This guide (for men) and reference (for women) will stretch you. My prayer is that you will be challenged and be better in your relationships starting today.

Enjoy,

PBW

DEDICATION

This book is dedicated to those who have believed and supported me throughout my life. This book is dedicated to my family who encourages me to be greater. This book is dedicated to couples, families, and individuals who are looking to improve themselves and their relationships. This book is dedicated to all those who cheered me on and inspired me to continuously write.

I also dedicate this book to my son, Nicholas. I love you, and I hope you read these words and apply them to your life and relationships. You used to see my letters and notes all over our home and asked why and what I was writing. I pray they soak in. I pray you will be better than me. I pray your journey is easier and more fulfilling than I can imagine. I pray that God protects you and that you keep a firm and sound mind when it's time to start dating, courting, and considering marriage. I pray you and your future wife find each other, love each other, protect each other, and pray with each other. I pray you practice more than I could ever preach.

ACKNOWLEDGEMENTS

I am beyond grateful for those who inspired and encouraged me to write this book, in addition to those who trust my advice and words to entertain and inform them. I want to thank all those who trusted me with their questions that became articles or words in this book. There were many nights I wanted to give up on this project due to failures of my own, but a lot of people encouraged me to push through. I thank you and please know that if I had the space to mention you all by name, I would.

I want to thank my mother, Jean Williams, for always writing to me even when I didn't feel like reading. The letters you sent were invaluable. I still have many. I love and thank you for accepting me at my best and worst. Thank you for your prayers and love.

I want to thank my father, Paul Williams, for the long conversations you think I wasn't listening to. I remember specific words of encouragement and your example of hard work! You always found a way and I live by that!

I want to thank Joseph Wilson for always being an available ear and resourceful voice. The word "mentor" doesn't serve what you mean to me. I am forever honored to be like a member of your own family.

I want to thank the men who received my work online and didn't judge it. You made it okay to continue to write because you knew I wasn't coming from an "I'm better than you" perspective. You gentlemen saw that I was walking beside you in this journey.

I want to acknowledge the relationships that didn't work for being the teaching tools of growth through experience, pain, and love. This is a formal apology for my shortcomings and imperfections. I take full responsibility for my part in the failure of the relationship.

I want to acknowledge and thank every person who ever shared my social media links, website, products, and posts. Thank you to my friends and family who cheered me on as Paul and support my work as Bashea, knowing I'm the same. My Middlebrook family, Red Storm/Front Page flag football family, East Tennessee State University family, and all new social media friends and family, you are appreciated!

TABLE OF CONTENTS

INTRODUCTION

I started writing *Dear Future Wife®* in the year 2001 after a failed relationship. I decided to confide in pen and paper because it was safe to share what I felt. In my notebook, I wouldn't be rejected. I was in full control of what I wanted to say, what I wanted to write, and how I felt. This did two things for me. It allowed me to connect with my ability to express true love while protecting it from those who had the ability to abuse it. Every letter was safe from that last breakup. At that time, I did not want to be emotionally connected because I was young, emotionally fragile, and immature. Plus, I was in college, and it seemed like most people weren't in relationships for the long haul. As I grew older, my goal for writing changed because I began to change. I lived out of protection. I felt the need to protect my heart, mind, and more importantly, my EGO. Whenever I felt like I was falling in love, I thought the girl or woman in my life would do something that showed me she wasn't ready. However, I eventually realized that the truth was that I was the one who wasn't ready because I had not yet healed. At times, I chose women who spoke to my pain or failure in the form of covering those issues. I had an open wound and my pen and pad were Band-Aids. I actually did not give them the power to be Band-Aids yet. They were emotional safety nets.

As I grew older, more mature, and closer to graduating college, the purpose of these letters evolved. I began to hold myself accountable, and I also actively worked to heal from broken and failed relationships. But that also got in the way because I held myself accountable to my letters as opposed to the relationships I pursued and was involved in. I was missing the person in front of me to be the me I wrote about.

After maturing and studying the mind and heart, I realized why my relationships still failed. I didn't understand that love varies and is different, depending on who is in the relationship, their beliefs and expectations. At the time of this revelation, I returned to my safe space of writing, but this time I shared my words with the world. It took a little while to share, but when I did, my anxiety was through the roof because I feared more rejection. I also feared my readers' expectations. I felt readers wanted the end results of my words as opposed to building authentic relationships with these words as a guide. I never wanted women to think these words were a ploy to get them. I never wanted men to think I was writing from a place of perfection and judgment of them. I wanted to make sure people didn't think I was hiding behind my words. These were all the thoughts that piled on top of dozens of other uncertainties that circled around the possible ramifications of releasing my words. What would people think? *Why is he soft? Is he selling dreams? Are these his words? Who is he writing to?* I never wanted to be or sound like one of those relationship dudes. Grammatical errors gave me heart palpitations. Then I got an unexpected response of "thank you." I was being thanked for helping others. I began to receive attention, but there was one problem. I didn't start writing to gain attention or let a woman know how I would love her. I wanted to express myself safely. I knew once again that paper doesn't reject. It doesn't take a mistake personal. I can just erase and redo. But people started telling me that my words were touching their souls and they were literally looking forward to love. Both men and women told me that I gave them new hope. I fought writing because the words got in the way of my relationships because many would read them and attach them to me instead of taking the words, advice, support, and encouragement and applying it to themselves or their relationships. <u>As you read this, ignore the writer and absorb the words for application.</u>

Purpose

The purpose of this book is to give readers realistic goals to apply to your current or future romantic love. We have to understand what love is to another person after mastering what it is to us. We have to understand that true love is mastering our responses, especially when we do not receive love the way we anticipated. When we are attempting to love another person, we have to know that both individuals want to experience love, but we utilize different emotional, psychological, and physical paths to get there. This is a journey of unlocking abandoned love, rediscovering your ability to be available to love, redesigning future experiences and efforts around love, choosing to be restored after broken love, learning to lead and follow each other in love, reframing negative thoughts about love, and igniting a desire to love deeply. This book will initiate healing, provide traditional dating ideas, and serve as a guide for healthy relationships. **The letters are not just from me to my future wife. They are for women to set a standard and men to embrace what they were born with.** Men are born to pursue, protect, and provide for our women. I am not speaking of just finances, but we will get into that later in the book. This book provides hope for a second chance.

Declaration

Read this next paragraph twice—once in your head and once out loud. This will prepare you for all things relationship.

Dear Relationship,

I am not afraid of you. I am not afraid to be patient and wait for you. I am not afraid to pursue you. I am not afraid of staying and fighting for you. I am not afraid of walking away from you when it's not right. I am not afraid to take a break from you. I am not afraid to end my break to be vulnerable again. I am not afraid to say, "I do." I am not afraid to say, "I don't." I am not afraid to build you up. I am not afraid to invest in you unselfishly. I am not afraid to "wait" while in you. I am not in a rush. I am not going to wait forever. I am not afraid to start all over. I am not afraid for a fresh start. I am not afraid of the work. I am not afraid of being hurt. I am not afraid of being alone. I am not afraid of sharing my space. I am not afraid of being loved. I am not afraid! I am not afraid to tell my past "bye" and say "hello" to my present in order for my future to be the gift that I deserve. You are no longer my biggest fear!

Dear Relationship, you are welcome.

Now, read that out loud.

We should be able to sift through fears about love to determine what's real and what's fake. We need to understand the root of our fears, how we have been influenced negatively, and then make a conscious decision to go where we want to be. It's important for us to decide to really "work." Work on what we want to give and receive. Understand that there won't be a perfect love, but a purposeful one—meaning, our relationships may continue to grow and learn as we remain open to teach and vice versa.

Letters

These are letters that helped me get through what I experienced and healed me from what didn't work. These are letters of other people's experiences which they have shared with me. In these letters, I assess what is happening in the current relationship climate. *These are letters of hope, opportunity, and healing.* These letters are teaching tools. There is no place for blame because choosing [a relationship] is about accountability; staying [in that relationship] is a choice.

Too often, we have an answer to our failed relationships and we focus on the end while ignoring the steps we took that led to the failures and the steps we need to take so that we don't repeat the outcomes or our behaviors. These letters will provide answers and make sense of experiences for both men and women. Culturally, we have been broken while looking for a fix (or broken and we are looking for a fix) and because some of us have not had good examples or any examples at all, we are just trying to figure it all out by ourselves. These letters are to influence your emotional memory. Emotional memory is your most powerful memory. We forget and recover from physical pain more easily than we do emotional memory and emotional pain. Getting stung by a bee hurts for a short time, but getting your heartbroken, being lied to, manipulated, unappreciated, not acknowledged, cheated on, etc. can last a lifetime. Those feelings can prevent you from dating, trusting, and engaging with others. These letters will help you trust yourself regardless of the response from others. These letters will allow you to love and be loveable.

As I was writing these letters, I considered various circumstances, circumstances such as a woman feeling the love she pretended to have and a man no longer being afraid to love the way he didn't see his father love his mother. I want these letters to speak to your relationship goals and deepest desires for love. These are letters of purpose! After each letter, I include a perspective of my emotional placement and psychological mindset at the time of writing.

Participate

As you read these letters, I don't want you to see them as fairytale or ideals that are unattainable or unrealistic. I encourage you to absorb, embrace, participate and relate. After my brief explanation there will be an opportunity to take notes about what you received from it. I want you to ask yourself, **"How can I apply this to my singleness, dating, courting, or marriage?"** This will require you to do more than read or dream. This requires application and participation. Even if you don't agree with my thoughts, writing your own response will be therapeutic. Don't hold it in. Let it out. Let out your anger, happiness, frustration, or new perspectives. Stay present! I want you to **take it personal.**

In each letter, there will be an important question, and it will be beneficial to answer each one for yourself. Some of the chapters of this book are not letters at all. They are important observations or thoughts about relationships that we all need to consider.

One last thing: always remember that in order to see his or her heart, you will have to reveal yours.

DEAR FUTURE WIFE

PART 1:

Before

DEAR FUTURE WIFE

Chapter 1

EMOTIONAL MANSTRESS/MISTRESS

Too many times we allow or choose to give and gain access to people outside of our relationships. We share intimate details or just communicate too often or at inappropriate times. We have loose boundaries and communication with people other than our significant others.

"Mistress" has a few definitions, but I want to concentrate on two. The first is a woman who has power, authority, or ownership; one who has control over or responsibility for someone or something. The second is a woman who is having a sexual-extramarital affair with a married man. The two are related in that the woman has some power and it is demonstrated by a man's behavior. Now, this isn't to let the men off the hook, because I believe there is a such thing as a "manstress." It is the male equivalent of the mistress in that a man extends his attention, sex, love, and time to a woman that is married to someone else.

Let's talk emotions since some may say that they never cheated or had a physical/sexual relationship outside of the one with their significant others. Let's also talk about how an emotional mistress/manstress can be dangerous to your relationship. Do you have a friend of the opposite sex that you rely on emotionally because you can't tell your partner the things you share with him/her? It's innocent right? That person just "gets you," and you feel more comfortable telling him/her because it's just safer. You don't have to worry about being judged or it being used against you. It's an outside safe space until that space becomes more comfortable than your relationship. Let's give an example: you are struggling to communicate your needs to your partner because either you don't know how to express them, or your partner doesn't know how to receive them. Because of that, you lean on someone of the opposite sex to be heard. That person "gets" you and you start to rely on that person, emotionally, simply because you are frustrated with the lack of emotional intimacy from your partner and the other person actually listens. Soon, that person outside your relationship develops a sense of belonging and sometimes responsibility. The thought process may shift subconsciously, and the manstress/mistress may want (and expect) a bigger role or wonder if a "real" relationship may work between the two of you. You, as the person who is already in a committed relationship, may think the same thing. Eventually, you make fewer attempts to connect with your significant other and develop more reliance on the person(s) outside of your relationship. What began as sharing emotions becomes complaints about your partner. That disrupts and destroys your relationship with your significant other. If behavior like this continues, the emotional relationship may lead to a physical one.

I encourage you to make attempts to strengthen your relationship with your partner through counseling, seminars, workshops, books, and communication exercises. If you aren't willing to bring a third unbiased party in to mediate the communication deficit, then that person should not be a part of your emotional reliance. I am not advocating that you can't have friends that you care about; this is to say that boundaries need to be strong and communication needs to be tight with you and your partner. Ask yourself if you are communicating what you need or want. Ask your partner if she/he understands what you are trying to communicate. Too many times we allow outside forces in and that may cause us to be emotionally stretched and disconnected from our significant others. Again, this does not mean you should isolate yourself from friends or associates. This means be careful with who you rely on for emotional support.

Chapter 2

I Needed to Get Ready for You

Dear Future Wife,

My desire is to be everything you need me to be.
My goal is to be whatever you desire me to be.
I am not saying I will reach these goals, but I will try.
Before I even attempted to, I realized I needed to get ready for you.
I needed to be alone.
There was a time when I was hurt; I needed to heal.
There was a time when I wanted to play; I needed to get serious.
I hid my pain in the games I played.
I can only imagine the pain I would have caused you if you were one of those women with whom I played.
Not to let every woman off the hook…
There were some who played games with me and put me further in debt to my healing.
I needed to detox and focus on me and the games I played.
The sad part is that when I played, I was ignorant to the fact that although I really wanted to get serious, my pain wouldn't let me.
There was a time when I had distractions in my life that weren't conducive to a successful partnership.
I had to work on me.
There were loose ends that were holding on to their false hopes. They did things to hinder my progress and I allowed them.

There were times when I felt insufficient which resulted in dangerous self-preservation.
This self-preservation prevented me from being "available" and made me hard to reach and understand.
I was good at not showing face.
I looked at my flaws as weapons or shields to attack others.
I didn't want to be vulnerable.
Who I am, my recovery time, and self-discovery prepared my readiness.
I designed and developed a kingdom.
My kingdom ready for a queen.
I had to create my kingdom prior to crowning you as my queen.
I wanted you to be in awe when I placed that crown on your head.
I wanted you to experience the results of my hard work.
I wanted to demonstrate and reference evidence of what I built that was great and sustainable.
These examples will be a point of reference for you to know that I can and will apply the same work ethic to keep you happy and loved.
Let's build on this foundation.
Bring your crown to my kingdom, switch it out, and add some jewels that we will choose together.
I realize you were a queen before we met!
I just want to make you my personal queen without diminishing your accomplishments.
I apologize if I made you wait long, and I appreciate your patience.
Your patience was evident without push or force that would normally push and force me to walk away from you.
Your patience was my water as I traveled across a desert.

PERSPECTIVE

As I wrote this, I realized that to reach a place of readiness, we need to address our issues, heal from our pasts, renew and restore our minds, bodies, and souls. We need to literally clean out the images and experiences that are holding us hostage. We also need to prepare to pursue or to be pursued, date, court, and marry. Our thoughtful preparation does not mean that we discredit what we have previously learned; it means that we focus on the lessons as opposed to the damages.

Think about the relationship that you remember the most. This is what I call emotional memory. How is that impacting you right now? Is that a relationship you want to repeat?

TAKE IT PERSONAL

The relationship I remember the most is my relationship to my late ex-husband. It impacts me because I remember how he treated me and how I was his queen. It is the example I look for in my relationships since then. I want some parts of it, but can do without other parts.

Dear Future Wife

Chapter 3

I'm Not Perfect

Dear Future Wife,

Allow me to introduce myself.
I am Mr. Imperfect.
I am happy to give you the results of all my corrected mistakes.
I have learned from my previous experiences in life, love, and relationships.
I'm forsaking my old ways and giving life to what makes me a better man.
I have realized that I will always be working to get better for you and for us.
I will make new mistakes, correct those, and continue to grow as your husband.
I understand that I will mess up, come up short, and disappoint you.
I understand that I will forget things like important dates.
I may forget your birthday, our anniversary, to pick up your favorite candy, or to do the laundry.
But there are things I will never forget.
I will never forget how to make you laugh and smile.
I will never forget how we met.
Most importantly, I will never forget how to love you.
I am imperfect, but I am not a quitter.
I realize a relationship and my personal growth require stamina.
I am always "in the gym!"
I understand there are no quick fixes in becoming a better man.
My motivation comes from within and is externalized by the way I treat you.

I will forever be improving while thanking you for your forgiveness and patience.
I will not concentrate on your flaws to distract me from my own.
I am imperfect while continually striving to be better for what you deserve.

PERSPECTIVE

It is important for us men to realize that we will never be perfect nor will there be a perfect time. I had to tell myself that there will never be a "perfect" time. There will always be things to work on. We can't let our processes stifle relationship progress. I think we as men feel like the timing has to be "just right" because we don't value ourselves enough to date incompletely. We worry that she may need someone who is perfect while knowing it doesn't exist. It is important to put value in the work we are doing. She may be that final piece for us to get over the hump. She may finally be the peace we need.

To all men, I encourage you to open up so that you can give dating, courting, and (perhaps even) a marriage an opportunity. We can communicate that we won't be perfect but not take advantage of being flawed by using that as an excuse. What imperfections do you use as excuses? What imperfections scare you from revealing the true you? What are you waiting to get right? Do you think a woman can handle your imperfections? What are you willing to tolerate and not tolerate? Embrace being perfectly imperfect. Go get her!

TAKE IT PERSONAL

That I am a strong, Type A personality and controlling. That I dont know every thing and actually need help with some things. I hope a man can handle my imperfections but I am fearful of being too strong-minded for him. I am not willing to tolerate dishonesty, disrespect, lack of ambition, lack of communicat

DEAR FUTURE WIFE

Chapter 4

I've Never Been Married, but I've Had Several Divorces

We as people no longer know the difference between being in a relationship and being married. Why? Because we stopped waiting to do the things that were meant for marriage and we do them in our relationships instead. There isn't any pressure to get married because sometimes the only change is a last name. Marriage is supposed to change your life not how your relationship is perceived. Example: "I'm not going to keep doing this if we are not married," as opposed to, "I'm going to keep doing this when we get married."

The lines of relationship and marriage have become so close that they are often blurred. Women nor men know the real differences between the two anymore. Men are cloaking short-term intentions with long-term techniques and women are taking advantage of being courted with no intention of staying. Intentional assumptions have planned relationships before the first date has even occurred and forced compatibility has become the norm. People are "falling in love" without knowing the person they claim to feel so much affection for. So, in wake of romantic and relational realities, I pose this question: How many divorces have you had?

Psychological and emotional marriage occurs when you are mentally connected with someone with whom you are dating or in a relationship while operating in the mindset of being his or her husband or wife. The vicious cycle of needing to belong to someone in a more permanent fashion begins again. You find yourself planning your forever based on marriage potential and not based on what's in front of you. Sometimes the initial warning signs are blatantly present, but you ignore them hoping that things can and will change. And you tell yourself that life won't be the same if you don't have that person occupying your space of void.

The demise of your relationship prompts a series of analyzing thoughts that overtake your emotions, leaving you wondering what you did wrong, what you could have done to make that person stay, and if you are truly worthy of someone loving you the way you love them. You focus your emotions and attention on the flaws of your life rather than thinking on what you have the ability to improve.

When it comes to romantic relationships, the vetting process begins with you. You have to be ready and willing to learn and enjoy yourself before you add someone else in the picture. Psyching yourself out to believe that you must play marriage to get married is not healthy.

Having sex then breaking up means you have shared yourself with yet another person. Your body count has gone up and another sexual soul tie has been created. The honeymoon will be a formality because you two have already had many honeymoons as you passed the days away locked up in your unmarried love-nests. And of course, you both wanted to wait to have sex, but fear kept you feeling as if you needed to check out the full package before you agreed to keep it. There you are comparing your new love to your old and wondering how to move on but hold on at the same time. The truth is that you should be willing to learn your new partner when you get married and be open to new experiences. Teaching your lover how to show love to you physically shows a deeper level of intimacy.

Some would agree that getting married costs less than getting divorced. A lack of teamwork after a split brings more chaos, especially when a child is involved. The child's living situation gets stretched and they have to almost choose a side. The child becomes the "middle man" bridging the gap of the father and mother falling out of each other's lives for good.

Just think, children witness it all and probably feel the strongest about the situation, yet they have no say so. They are just required to go where the wind (or the judge) blows them.

Divorces occur when two people live together, have sex, have children, share bills, then, for whatever reason, they breakup. Assets must be separated and then there's the daunting task of deciding who gets what— who stays in the house, who keeps the dog, who gets the kids and when, and so on. Everything the two of you built together gets torn down the middle or torn apart altogether.

And the love you thought you shared disappears.

Think about these things before you make marriage investments in a boyfriend or girlfriend. Be patient and protect your sanity at all costs. Stay in the moment of the relationship and allow it to grow before you enter into an illegitimate marriage. Be willing to leave something to look forward to and some things to work towards. If your partner isn't willing to wait or work for a marriage, then they aren't the one for you. There is a way of showing yourself without giving all of yourself. From the words of Ms. Janet Jackson, "Let's wait awhile before it's too late." Don't add another divorce to your collection. Wait to build a real marriage.

DEAR FUTURE WIFE

Chapter 5

RE-LEARN

Dear Future Wife,

I started out a gentleman but grew lazy and forgetful.

I used to open the door without even thinking about it.

I used to schedule a date, plan it out, and execute it.

I used to take your coat from you and either hang it up or put it behind your chair.

I used to have no problem holding your purse, if need be.

I used to go to the store for myself and leave out with more items for you.

I used to consider your emotions before making a decision.

Flowers? They were a monthly thing at a minimum.

I used to wake up and think, "What can I do today to show her she is appreciated?"

I lost that.

Chivalry was dead. Chivalry was killed. Chivalry was fought with ego. Chivalry was buried.

It happened for many reasons:

I lost value in your beauty and what you deserved.

You didn't hold me up to that standard.

According to the world, "thirst" replaced traditional, genuine, old-school pursuing.

Rejection was tied to my ego and it didn't allow me to be vulnerable.

I got comfortable with how everyone else moved.

I allowed the "independent" woman to diminish my ability to be strong, to be a provider.

I lost touch of self and what a man is to a woman.

I have been "lazy," dating in comfort and with little effort.

Women thought, "There are too many of us and if I challenge him, I will lose him."

I knew that and relied on the numbers game.

Then you told me, "NO!"

No, it isn't going to be easy.

I am going to have to work for it.

I bucked and walked initially, but turned around, because I needed and wanted you.

I also understood standards.

I respected yours.

I had flashbacks of how I was taught that women were to be treated like custom-made diamonds.

I took my time to invest in you.

I applied patience and didn't force anything.

I paid attention to what you liked and catered to it.

I "uniquely" dated you; my steps were specific to you.

I provided consistency.

I was decisive.

I healed from my previous experiences.

I was present—physically, mentally, and emotionally.

I brought the gentleman back and stood so proud that your heart softened due to my efforts.

Things became fun again.

We took away the pressure.

We smiled at each other.

I treated you without counting my money or expecting a return.

You surprised me with, "Let me get this one."

Chivalry is back. I pinky promise.

I relearned how valuable you are and the value in courting you.

I helped you out of the car.

RE-LEARN

I pumped the gas and paid for it.
I made sure your car was washed and the maintenance on it was up-to-
date.
All you had to do was drive it.
I opened your doors.
Chivalry is back. I promise.

PERSPECTIVE

When I wrote this, I realized relearning how to be a gentleman was a part of my preparation. I needed to do this so that I could get ready to date again with purpose of starting, building, and sustaining a relationship. We men have become comfortable with little effort because many women have made it effortless. When we meet a woman that says "no" or requires more, we naturally gravitate to what (and who) doesn't challenge us. In reality, we don't want the "just in case/fall back" woman for the long term; we just accept that person for "right now." There is another side to it. Old-fashioned chivalry is devalued by women and frowned upon in society. These gestures seem extra and sometimes too hard to maintain.

Fellas, why is it so difficult to be chivalrous? What is preventing you from doing the things to show a woman you care? What's realistic for you to give and receive? Women, has chivalry become corny or does it take away from your womanhood or independence?

TAKE IT PERSONAL

_____

_____

_____

_____

_____

_____

_____

Chapter 6

ABOUT THE FIGHT

Dear Future Wife,

I used to love our conversations.

Our conversations were soft-flowing, easy, supportive, and educating.

We could talk about everything. We could have an entire conversation in our sleep and wake up like we never left off.

We used to say what we meant with confidence, now we say what we mean while saying it mean.

We used to be able to listen to what the other had to say, now we just listen for the moment the other person gets quiet so we can be heard.

We would talk all day now we avoid talking all day because the purpose used to be to see how the other is doing; now we talk to make sure we know what the other person is doing.

We used to want to give the other access to our emotions; now we don't know how to control our emotions.

One thing we know how to do is fight.

Tragically, now when we walk away from the fight we can't figure out what has kept us connected in the first place.

Then we fight some more. This time there were no visible adversaries. We kept looking around with emotional fists clutched.

We felt a swing that missed. It was the wind, because we couldn't pinpoint where the attack came from. So, we were able to sustain our positions in our walk away.

Then something happened; we felt a hit.

Contact!

It was ourselves who we couldn't dodge, and the hook was a realization that our external battle was in an internal war that realized we were arguing with ourselves while aiming at each other. We were the same person.

While walking parallel but facing the opposite direction; we made a turn. I turned left, and she turn right, and the two lines became a circle. We realized we complimented each other and our fight should have been holding hands against the past that held us back all while determining our present steps toward the future.

PERSPECTIVE

Think about a time when you were having a conversation, debate, argument, or fight, and all you could focus on was protecting, hurting, getting your point across, and trying to convince someone else to agree with you. What was it really about? Sometimes we don't know how to say, "I just want to feel like we are on the same page, going in the same direction, trusting each other, believing in each other, and hearing each other…"

In the beginning, it's okay to disagree because you accept the fact that you are learning that person and you are willing to get to know him or her. In the beginning you commit to listening. As time goes by, your guard falls down in one area, but your defenses increase. How is that? You've become more vulnerable because you have allowed him or her in. When your partner doesn't accept your emotional vulnerability, you think he or she is disagreeing for a different reason, but the reality is that this person is still learning you. What would happen if you accepted that there is no time limit on learning you and vice versa. Not every disagreement should be a fight, not every disagreement means that your partner isn't on your team. You can disagree and still be for/with each other. What is behind the fight?

TAKE IT PERSONAL

_____

_____

_____

_____

_____

_____

_____

DEAR FUTURE WIFE

Chapter 7

CAN I BE VULNERABLE?

Dear Future Wife,

A man's armor is thicker than steel.
To his detriment, once penetrated, it's never quick to heal.
Layers of protection make it hard to reveal.
The softer side, oftentimes, he's not willing to deal.
Strong, battle-tested approved with a seal.
That's why we show straight face, until (we know) it's real.
We can't imagine you (not) understanding what we consider a done deal.
We want to be vulnerable with you but want you to understand it doesn't mean we are weak.
We want to be able to depend on your softness to lessen the blows of our falls.
We want to be able to share our darkest moments, trusting you to be a light.
We want to be better for you, despite society's cliché description of a man being unable to be vulnerable and emotionally available.
We want to be what you need, not what's popular and caters to your desire.
We want to show you that it is necessary to keep you secure in your walk which is the complete understanding of…"We are our lady's man."
We want you to share the moments and express that "you succeeded in your efforts of finding me" when we failed at something else.
We want to know that our days of external struggle and coming up short of pleasing the world will not translate into internal failure to you.

We don't want to compete at home.
We don't want to compete with the naturalization of a man's order.
A man's "end all."
A man's verbal "be all."
We do not desire additional competition.
Please don't compare our rare (vulnerability) to something that isn't consistent with your desire.
Nor do we compare it to the so-called "normal man."
We continue to switch to a pleasing position as a reminder to keep you emotionally occupied and happy.
There are many facets of a woman that we ignore, and we acknowledge the work that needs to be done.
We put ourselves in positions to apologize.
We often make the mistake of apologizing to make you okay in order to keep the environment quiet.
We repent for thinking that it's okay to say things we really didn't mean.
We embrace the thought of enjoying the moment but absorb the truth of a lifetime.
We want to say "hello," while being emotionally naked and offer it with no surprises.
How will you take that?
How are your responses shaped by your experiences?
How are your responses shaped by what society has told you?
Our connection with being vulnerable is tied to our trust in you.
Did we make a mistake???
Can we say, "I need your essence," without you telling us, "You will not succeed without my presence?"
Can we tell you we are afraid?
Can we say we don't know?
Can we be silent and hope it works out?
I am "bodyguard" strong for you, and I need you to be "bulletproof" supportive of me.
Can we say, "I failed, and I am sorry," without you calling us sorry?
Let's talk…

Perspective

Vulnerability is so tough. We aren't raised to be "vulnerable," and when we are, and it isn't handled properly, because of that our future expressions of vulnerability are limited. We protect ourselves. We don't give our women many opportunities to experience or see our vulnerable sides. We think, *what will she do with it? What's the worst that can happen?* The truth is that we are fighting the world and don't want the fight to live in our lives forever.

Men, what will it take for you to be vulnerable? How would you want a woman to handle your vulnerability? Women, what is allowed? What can you handle?

Take it Personal

_____

_____

_____

_____

_____

_____

_____

_____

DEAR FUTURE WIFE

Chapter 8

MY FANTASY

Dear Future Wife,

I have been asked to share my fantasy when it comes to sexual relations.
When it comes to sex, what have I never done?
What positions haven't I tried?
What places haven't I indulged?
How many partners at a time?
What is beyond my wildest imagination?
If I could be with anyone, who would I choose?
What is off limits?
What are my desires?
What type of music would I play while pleasuring her?
Have I had any complaints?
Have I made someone cry during a sexual encounter?
The questions came, and I didn't know how to answer them genuinely.
I felt uncomfortable answering them, not because I was in doubt, not because these women may or may not have experienced some of these scenarios, but because something was missing.
I was not aligned with my ultimate fantasy— that's what was missing.
My ultimate fantasy remained the same.
I wanted answers to be answered by my wife.
My fantasy is to start my connection of souls, sexually, with my wife.

It starts with saying "I do!"
Then, on our honeymoon, being totally free.
Free from guilt.
Free from wondering *is she the one.*
Free from releasing my efforts to embrace someone who may not be my forever.
Scared that my performance made more sense and held more weight than our covenant.
I wanted to create love, make love, and live in love without doubts of tomorrow's dislikes.
Dislikes that create, make, or live in a goodbye that could be so easily said.
I want to look in your eyes during each love-making moment and make our soul-tie even tighter.
A knot that could never be untied.
My fantasy starts with "I do."
My fantasy is to travel to an exotic island, be greeted with, "Welcome, Mr. and Mrs., here is your room."
My fantasy is to hear someone say, "You have a beautiful wife."
My fantasy is to introduce you in this exact way, "This is my wife."
My fantasy is to wake up one day and have a moment in awe because, "I'm married."
My fantasy is to not be the only "not married" man in a circle of my close friends.
My fantasy is to get married for all the right reasons.
My fantasy is us working on our issues despite the difficulties.
My fantasy is not giving up on each other.
My fantasy is for you to be able to channel your inner Shug Avery and say, "I's married now," and mean it.
My fantasy is to have the approval of God in line with what making love was made for.
My fantasy is for my wife to have all the answers.

PERSPECTIVE

Let's be honest. We desire sex and we are thinking about it. As we are working on ourselves, it is important to plan and address what sex should be for and to us. It's healthier to plan and shape our fantasies while tying them to a relationship, as opposed to making a relationship out of sex. Yes! There is a possibility that we can be in a relationship for the rest of our lives, and this *could* alleviate drama.

Here are some questions to consider: What drama comes with sex outside of a relationship or even marriage? Those "arrangements" don't last long. What do 'situationships' block? What will happen when either of you wants to pursue someone *else* long-term?

Guys, how many times have you heard a woman say, "But, I gave you my body and you're acting like this!?" Ladies, how many times have you said that?

TAKE IT PERSONAL

_____

_____

_____

_____

_____

_____

_____

DEAR FUTURE WIFE

Chapter 9

SUITED AND DRESSED UP HEARTS

There seems to be a shift in how we operate today. We are still willing to give our time to people of interest, and yet there is a detachment or separation of sorts. The order of connecting with someone has changed. What used to be first is now an afterthought. What was once a condition to obtain physical penetration is now an optional choice that is seldom selected and even less frequently met. I am talking about the heart. It used to be the key to intimacy, but now it is protected by giving our naked bodies. How did we get here? How did we get to the point where our naked bodies serve as shields to emotion and vulnerability? *Are you willing to undress your heart before you take off your clothes?*

Our hearts are stubborn due to what we have experienced in the past after we've made the choice to share them. We walk around physically free, but our emotions are in bondage. Subconsciously, we are saying, "You can have my body, but you can't have my heart. You can enter me without penetrating my heart."

We have convinced ourselves that it's not safe to take risks with our hearts or put our hearts in harm's way. Although the heart is the body's strongest organ, we refuse to exercise it. Some of us are literally conducting self-talks like, "Don't catch feelings, you already know what it is." Or, "Just give him/her your body and the heart will come around later." This often results in increasing your "body count" and further disconnecting from your heart. When we prepare to lay down, we throw our clothes on the floor, and stand there naked and detached because we have left our hearts in the car.

When did it become easier to give your body away than to share your heart? Or the better question is: why have we allowed this to be the norm?

Broken hearts have led to broken norms in society. "Detachment-sex" is the norm until we don't get what we want. When the relationship doesn't go our way, we think, "But, how could you leave me? I gave you my body!" The real question should be: "What are you doing with my heart?" Even those who are having sex are not taking the time to explore the wants and needs of their partners. Instead, they are making assumptions about what pleases their partners based on previous sexual encounters. If we took the time to really get to know a potential partner, the sex would be emotionally amazing as opposed to emotionally draining. Because of impatience, learning the mind, body, and soul has been replaced with selfish goals that are only aimed at finishing. Before we lay down, we should make the heart connection with our partners and this should continue long after we get up.

There is a "community of wait." This is the community that is practicing abstinence or celibacy. I found out that for myself and many others in this community, we were going about this process of connecting all wrong. We'd made it about us or the person we were choosing not to sleep with. But rather, the focus of the wait, should be to create a closer connection to God and prepare for the person God has for us. Some of us still protected our hearts even when we didn't give our bodies. We used "waiting" as a badge of honor, but we were also waiting to connect with someone emotionally and spiritually. Withholding sex is great, but are we willing to unfold our hearts to connect? Ask yourself *what is the purpose of the wait*? While waiting are you repairing yourself or are you abstaining from sex to protect yourself from another failed relationship? Sex is off the table, but is your heart on the table? There is pressure to give in to fit in and find love but stay strong. Someone will respect your desire to be heart and spirit led.

Be willing to undress your heart.

SUITED AND DRESSED UP HEARTS

Be willing to be touched – not just physically, but within your mind, heart, and spirit. Be willing to let someone discover the parts of you that you keep locked away. It's easy to take your clothes off, but difficult to undress your heart. I know it's challenging, but remember your heart is strong and it needs exercise. Allow it to be touched. Wait on physical penetration until the person you are with is willing to connect, protect, and cover your heart as if it were their own. Be available to share your heart. This doesn't mean you should give your heart to any and everyone you meet but take the time to learn people who have potential. Really invest in love! Remember that feelings aren't taught, but the reactions to feelings are. Will you be proactive or reactive with your heart? Will you play the offense or defense?

DEAR FUTURE WIFE

Chapter 10

PURSUING YOU

Dear Future Wife,

There are two ways a man pursues a woman. She's either a "job" or a "career."

A job is temporary; something just to hold you over until you find something else—something better.

A job is something you need right now to pass the time, add to the resume, a quick work, etc.

A career is something in which you invest, where you want to be, extends the definition of you, where you want to be purposely, and the results of hard work etc.

Don't get me wrong, a job can eventually turn into a career, but it just wasn't pursued the same way. Gaining a career from that job wasn't the intention.

I am blessed that you reviewed my application carefully.

You saw that I checked single as my marital status.

While pursuing you, I am not married, engaged, involved, or playing the fence on what I want for the rest of my life.

When I clicked single, it didn't mean I was available to others.

I am single, looking for a double, which results in us becoming a married couple.

I took my time with my application, because I want you long-term.

I worked to get to where you are, and I want to be beside you.

I didn't lie on my resume!

My experiences have shaped me into who I am.
Who I am is a man ready to grow in the position of your husband.
While reviewing my resume, don't be deterred.
I will share my experiences of past relationships when appropriate.
Don't worry!
My love for you is not defined or shaped by how others have mismanaged it.
You will experience a love I have never been able to give because my resume experiences don't contain my future; they just influenced and prepared it.
I am ready for on-the-job training. I am ready to move up. I am ready to retire in love with you.
Will you hire me?
Hire me for the long haul. Our relationship will be my career; my jobs have begun and ended.
I am living in our greatest accomplishment.
Will you hire me to always work hard, overachieve, and grow our company?
I am working to get noticed and chosen among the applicants.

PERSPECTIVE

Keep in mind, we are no longer looking for quick relationships. We are looking for that end goal, the WIFE. If that is where we are then we need to be intentional in every sense of the word. The words WIFE and FOREVER should mean the same thing. What work are you willing to do, sacrifice, etc.? How do those terms affect the pursuit?

TAKE IT PERSONAL

_____

_____

_____

_____

_____

_____

_____

_____

_____

DEAR FUTURE WIFE

Chapter 11

FIVE WAYS A WOMAN NEEDS TO FEEL PROTECTED

In order for a woman to take a man seriously and really give him a chance, she needs to feel protected. There are things a man can do to make her feel that way. Men, this doesn't mean you have to stand in front of a bullet or fight every man that either of you feels threatened by. She needs to feel secure mentally, emotionally, spiritually, financially, and physically. I personally feel protecting her spiritually is most important.

She needs to feel that when she steps out into the world, her man has her back. She needs to know wherever she feels weak, he makes her strong. There is a look a woman gives you when she knows you can handle whatever may be ahead of the two of you.

Here are a man's guide (and a woman's reference) to five ways a woman needs to feel protected, and it is up to us men to step up the plate.

1. **Mentally.**

A woman's thoughts need to be safe in your response. This will be evident by your ability to listen and understand. She needs to feel you're mentally connected and thoughtfully stimulated by her thinking. Being able to express what she is thinking to you and you letting her know it makes sense. She will ask and wait for your response.

She needs to know that you are hearing her, but more importantly, listening to her. Her thought process needs to be mirrored in that you reflect and project her thinking. The question of, "Are you thinking what I am thinking?" will be displayed through your actions. There will be disconnects, and in those disconnects, she needs to be able to trust that you understand why she is thinking differently. You don't always have to agree, but understanding where she is coming from is admirable and desired.

P.S.- Don't call her crazy for thinking that.

2. **Emotionally.**

There is a thought and understanding that men are more logical, and women are more emotional. With that being said, we can NOT devalue what women feel. A tear isn't the end of the world. An emotional moment isn't always a major cause for concern. Hug her and let her know it's okay.

You may need patience for some moments, especially during that special time of the month. We have to learn to embrace their change in emotions. We have a unique ability of not "taking it personal," but we don't have to show them what they are going through emotionally is too much for us to deal with. They already understand; well somewhat.

I am not describing the unstable women. If they are cycling through emotions consistently, then it may be too much for them to manage and impossible for you to manage. Don't make them feel inferior by attacking them emotionally. If it is too much and you have or need to exit, do it with class.

P.S. - In the same way we get attached to them emotionally when they are happy, we must connect to their emotions when they are unhappy.

3. **Spiritually.**

Can you cover her? Can you take her hand and pray with and for her? Before you pick up the fork to eat, pick up her hand and bless the food. Provide an example of what a spiritual man looks like and is. This does not mean be a preacher or be extra religious by following a tradition. This is about having an evident relationship with God and incorporating her into your beliefs.

Does she see and feel your prayers?

She needs to know that before you make big decisions in your life your time alone in prayer will influence and lead you. She needs to know that everything will be alright because you have intimate conversations with God. She needs to be able to trust that you trust God and exercise FAITH. She needs to feel the aura of a higher calling that she can't describe. Your ability to pray will produce trust.

P.S. - When a man identifies a woman's insecurities, he has two options: pray over them or prey on them.

4. **Financially.**

This isn't about living beyond your means or paying for everything. This isn't about paying her bills or buying her anything she wants. This is about being financially trustworthy and responsible. Can you manage your own money? Can you manage a checkbook, credit card, and your cash?

This is about financial maintenance. Can you make the BEST option when you are faced with a major financial decision? Can you say, "Hey, I know we have it but let's exercise patience." Will you be able to consider credit? Can you say, "Let's build our savings individually so that when we decide to get married, we have a substantial amount in an account for an emergency."

What does your retirement look like? Can you help her get hers in order? What does your debt look like? Can you provide resources for her to utilize to match yours (if you're winning in this area)?

When she makes more than you, are you still secure? Can you still operate in a leadership role? Remember, you aren't defined by your financial status. What if she has it all together and you don't? Can she trust you to allow her to lead you and show you the way because there are many women who have learned to manage their money better than men? She needs to know that you are secure in your financial status or growth. Can you clearly define your financial plan?

P.S.- Income isn't as important as money management.

5. **Physically.**

We have to be able to stand tall and make her feel safe. This has nothing to do with height or stature. This has everything to do with confidence. Don't confuse confidence and being sure with arrogance. We will need to decide and understand that our position in manhood isn't defined by brawn. We should mature in our idea of domination from being a quick-tempered boy to a thoughtful and calculated man. We need to understand the consequences of our actions. We should focus on long-term.

We need to understand danger. We have to be able to tell the woman in our lives, "That isn't a good idea. Trust me; it isn't safe." We need to be strong in walking away from a situation that isn't conducive to our safety.

As a man, if you are in a situation where you are physically challenged, responding physically isn't always the way to protect her. At some point in your life, "protection" is knowing when to walk away or when to apologize without blaming. If your woman does not understand that, then she may not be the one for you. At some point, you have to realize you are too old to be putting up the dukes.

Walking on the outside. Putting on her coat. A firm embrace. A confident kiss. Holding her hand and exchanging energy. Not being passive to outsiders. Stopping her from crossing the street when she didn't look. Her watching you take a strong stance is a complete turn-on. Taking a firm position on a decision—this is protection.

P.S. - She should not be testing your childhood wrestling, boxing, MMA, or Ninja skills at any time.

Chapter 12

I LOVE YOUR STRENGTH

Dear Future Wife,

I love your independence. I honor your journey and accomplishments.
You've done so much without the help of a man.
You go girl!
I see and marvel at how strong you are and at what you've become.
I just need you to understand that I'm the man. I'm your man and you
can't always walk bedside me. Sometimes you NEED to get behind me.
I say this because I want and need to protect you from what's in front of
us. Allow me to be your armor.
Don't confuse the word "role" with "rule;" they are different.
You're still a strong woman; now you just have me as a force field.
Sometimes I NEED to walk behind you, because you are stronger than me
in an area. I am okay with that. I love your strength. When this happens, I
am still a man! More importantly, I am your man!
We will find balance during our creation process. Your strength will cover
my weakness. My strength will cover your weakness. The plan is to cover
each other.
We walk side-by-side at times and one in front of the other at times.
The position may change, but together, we will remain.
I love your strength.
You ready? Let's go get 'em!

Your strength doesn't intimidate me.
I love it because it has allowed you to become what I love.
Hopefully you won't use your strength against me.
Against me to hold me at bay. Against me to keep me away. Against me to push me away.
I don't want to fight your strength; I want to fight beside your strength.
Resiliency and restoration allowed us to meet here and I want to stay.
I see what you have accomplished, and I see that you are a woman who not only knows what she wants but knows how to get it.
I am a man who knows what he wants and knows how to get what he wants!
I want you and your strength. I am strong enough to compliment your strength and protect you.
I love your strength, so let's work out together!

PERSPECTIVE

The thoughts behind this letter were based on the idea (that some believe) that a strong woman is intimidating to a man. Once a man is secure in himself, he admires a strong woman because she can stand tall beside him and also share the lead. Sometimes "you're too strong" is confused with you aren't flexible and are unwilling to compromise. Both are key to a healthy relationship and communication.

Men: ask yourself what about a woman's strength is valuable and what is too much to manage. Women: ask yourself what is behind your strength and what is protecting you from opening your heart and preventing you from connecting with a true suitor? Is strength a mask or an asset to your healthy relationship opportunities?

TAKE IT PERSONAL

_____

_____

_____

_____

_____

_____

_____

DEAR FUTURE WIFE

Chapter 13

IT'S TIME TO START
DATING WITH PURPOSE

Ladies...

Please accept this sincere apology and genuine promise to date you with purpose.

We, men, realize we have been going about this courting endeavor all wrong, when in fact what we attempted could be called "courting."

We have not been what men who seek wives need to be. We have not been the example of what a real man needs to be for a woman. As individuals, we have not been what a husband should and needs to be to his wife. We have made mistakes and we want to take the time to make things right.

We are starting with ourselves by taking ownership of what we have and have not been doing as the leader. After taking ownership, we are apologizing. After apologizing, we are planning. We plan to change our ways. We will implement our plans to be what we were designed to be and that is the man of your life.

Even if you don't choose us, we want you to see how we have changed by showing you what you deserve. We will get back to traditional and purposeful courtship and relationships.

It starts with us, men.

Ownership.

We have failed you. Whether we have excuses or reasons for our behavior, we are taking ownership. We are not blaming our fathers, mothers, societies, friends, nor our past pain for what and who we used to be. We are changing.

When our fathers were good examples, we allowed the pain of our past to dictate how we treated you. We allowed society to be our real teacher while fathers took on the substitute's role. We ignored our father's teachings. We never grew as men and, instead, maintained our boyish/childish ways.

When our fathers weren't there, we weren't taught how to be men, lovers, or genuine friends. Sometimes, they showed us the player lifestyle. Fathers disappeared at some point in life and there were no male figures to whisper or yell to us, "That isn't how you handle a woman's heart." Fathers weren't there to show us how to love the women in our lives. Fathers showed us how to hurt the mothers of our children while remaining smooth enough to have our cakes and eat them, too.

We, men, admit that.

While moms were present, we didn't really trust them simply because they were our mothers. We felt like they had to guide us with or give us a directive on relationships just because it was part of their roles as parents. Just like they had to tell us to take the trash out when we were young, but ultimately when we move out, we decided if we would take it out or not. We didn't genuinely accept their guidance. We had the wrong idea like, "What does mom know about how to be a man to a woman?"

We wanted to maintain our boyish/childish ways. We wanted to have fun while not paying attention to the pain we were causing. We held on to, "I will change once I am engaged or married." We ignored the fact that Mommy was too embarrassed to tell you to leave her son before we hurt you.

On the other hand, some mothers never showed how they expected to be loved. Some mothers never sat us down to say, "This is how you treat women." Mothers never said, "Treat her like you would want a man to treat me." Mothers never said, "Treat women like you would want the women in your family to be treated. Mothers never walked away from being treated poorly by the men in their lives. We ignored the tears behind their smiles.

We, men, admit that.

Society has constantly shown men that it's cool to have several women at one time: that it's a sport to juggle multiple relationships. Every day we learned how to be a player and we sat in the front rows of our classes to catch the lessons. We applied those teachings to our lives and excelled or at least tried. Society has taught men that being with multiple women is cool, being chivalrous is corny, and being loyal is outdated. Men were told to be fruitful and multiply. We were told that a man was not made to be monogamous.

Men listened to society and put value in what we were taught as opposed to how you thought of us. Men let society dictate what beautiful was and held you to those standards.

We, men, admit that.

Man's Pain Is...

Pain that you weren't responsible for, but we held you accountable… Pain from our pasts… we have adopted pain, and we even have some imaginary pain. I say "imaginary" because we avoid the pain by inflicting it on you first. I say "adopted" because we act as if the pain our friends, brothers, and other male counterparts have experienced were ours as well.

These pain points allowed men to prepare for anyone planning on hurting us first. I can admit, we sometimes expected you to hurt us. We expected you to pay us back for what we did to previous women, and we expected to be that guy who got played. We got you before you got us, even though you never intended or planned to hurt us.

We took advantage of you being "cool" and treated you like one of the fellas emotionally. We put your feelings and emotions in the friend zone but put your body in the sex zone.

We didn't care about the impact it would put on the men that came behind us. The next man suffered because of what the last man did to you. We take responsibility and apologize.

Apology.

We have a lot of apologizing to do and we are here to admit that in hopes that we can move forward. We apologize for not being who we were designed to be and that is a man of integrity, honesty, and loyalty.
We apologize for behaving as if we didn't ask you to be our lady.
We apologize for saying "I do" and continuing to do the things we did before we got married.
We apologize for not allowing your heart to leave or recover when we knew we didn't really want, deserve, or cherish you.
We apologize for holding you hostage with our words and selfish intentions.
We apologize for using sex to tie your soul to what we wanted.
We apologize for apologizing with sex.
We apologize for making the notches on our belts a competition and celebration with our boys.
We apologize for creating the thought that you dressing sexually is okay and it is what we desire.
We apologize for allowing skimpy clothes to be the only way to gain our attention.
We apologize for getting good at sex and using it to define us.
We apologize for not taking the effort to know you and instead putting our efforts in knowing how to please you sexually.
We apologize for hiding our personality behind our wallets.
We apologize for attempting to buy you.
We apologize for knowing we weren't ready but going forward anyway.
We apologize for taking advantage of the women-to-men ratio, being womanizers because you outnumber us.
We apologize for using your insecurities to our advantage.
We apologize for influencing your pain and attitude in a negative way.
We apologize for saying we "love you" when not even being sure if we liked you.

We apologize for using your desire to be married as a desire to be carried.
We apologize for never emotionally maturing.
We apologize for leading you, only to let you down.
We apologize for trying to figure things out and leaving you feeling like we were using you as a test dummy for the one we really wanted.
We apologize for using your mind, body, and soul instead of catering to them.
We apologize for the tears we caused to run down your face.
We apologize for abandoning you.

Plan.

Now that we, men, have that off of our chests, we will be different.
We will go over our plan daily and change our approach.
We will not apply our plan until we know we are ready.
We will be real, clear, consistent, and present.
We will consider all of you when we make decisions to pursue you.
We will consider the expectation we have of how we expect our daughters to be treated.
We will consider how we want our sons to treat their future female friends, girlfriends, and wives.
We will be what our fathers taught us or what we expected from them as the leaders.
We will lead with care.
We will be what our mothers deserve(d). We will be what they taught us to be as men to our women.
We will date you with the purpose of forever.
We will earn your trust and keep it.
We will treasure your heart.
We will stay connected to your emotions.
Instead of telling you our plan, we will show you.

Dear Future Wife

PART 2:

DEAR FUTURE WIFE

Chapter 14

SECURE IN MY ARMS

Dear Future Wife,

I need you to be secure.

I need you to know that the same traits that attracted you are also attractive to other women.

That does not mean their attraction will lead me to where they and I meet.

That does not mean I am attracted to their attraction.

I need you to know my efforts and just because my efforts are spread across multiple assignments it does not decrease your value.

I need you to know my attention will never exist outside of what we want for each other and our relationship.

I need you to know that other women will inspire me.

Wait, before you allow insecurity to run wild in your thoughts and emotions…

Know that no matter where my inspiration comes from, you will receive my dedication.

The beginning of me existed before we met, and I want the ending of me to expire while we are together.

Every single day will be a meeting of US.

I will be loved by others but will only LOVE ON YOU.

Me saying "hello" to other women does not mean I'm telling you or my promises to us GOODBYE.

I am not inviting anyone past the security of our relationship.

This relationship is V.I.P. and the P is singular. You are that person who is very important to me.

The ideas behind my thoughts may not always derive from you.

They may come from other women.

That does not mean you are lacking in any area of our lives together.

That just means another woman said or did something that sparked a new way for me to please you.

I need you to be secure enough to know, believe, and feel that my passion exists in making you in awe of me.

I am not interested in an "awe" of interest from others.

Allow me to show you how rare you are to me.

How there isn't anyone comparable and how I will continue to work to keep you as my wife.

You will always know the significance in me saying the words, "I love you," by the way I LOVE YOU.

I accept the responsibility of influencing your security in our relationship.

Allow my arms to secure you from anything that may create doubt and everything that does not belong in our relationship. **You are secure in my arms.**

PERSPECTIVE

Insecurity destroys relationships. Whether these insecurities are valid, invalid, confirmed, or anticipated. There are so many opportunities for us men to confirm our commitment or her insecurities. Of course some women come into relationships experienced in disappointment, distrust, and/or damaged from what another did to them whether it came from fathers or other relationships. BUT we have a responsibility to be different and reassuring. Yes, we have a choice to walk away when we see signs of insecurity, but it is sometimes worth the effort to stay and show her something different. Even the way we walk away should be admirable. It isn't always about what she gets from the end, but our responsibility is still to be honorable. How has insecurity in yourself or partner impacted your relationships? What can you do to secure each other without compromising yourself?

TAKE IT PERSONAL

_____

_____

_____

_____

_____

_____

_____

_____

DEAR FUTURE WIFE

Chapter 15

YOU ARE MY SIDE PEACE

Dear Future Wife,

Figuratively speaking, there is a war going on, and I can't keep fighting alone.
I can't be the only one in the world trying to survive.
I can take on everything alone, but why should I when I know there is someone amazing that should be by my side?
My Side Peace.
I don't think we were created to be alone. To love alone.
To navigate without a partner for life.
The word "side" has been taught to be a bad thing when it comes to two people interacting.
We have abused what it means to be in wait, support, or supplemental.
I fell for it when I heard the term "side piece."
I watched a video of how someone described it as men being misinformed because we disrespected our "main" in order to have a side piece.
After really thinking about that concept, it didn't sit well with me, and I thought we were using a word that sounded right but had the wrong spelling.
Piece is a part, peace is stillness.
Piece is minimized, peace is maximized.
The Word I read said you were my rib, pulled from my side, and it didn't describe what it meant to now have your rib back.
It is left up to interpretation.

I thought to myself, why can't it mean pulled from my in "side" to be placed by my side?

This doesn't diminish my partner, instead it equalizes her so that I can step outside of myself to get support, another view, and additional balance.

While you are by my side, I recognize you as an equal, I am by yours.

I am your side peace.

So much to fight through, side peace.

So much to fight for, side peace.

By my side against the struggles of a walk that is often walked alone.

I'm not lonely; I just trust you as my ride along.

Dual correction, identical ideals of protection, you are, I am, we are what is needed in a teamwork's creation of perfection.

I can't imagine the idea of side peace being described as less than a duplication of me that gives additional perspective.

A woman's intuition to a man's vision is beyond what I can think when PEACE is created.

When I have a hard day, coming home to my Peace.

When you are faced with anything that's unsettling, coming home to your Peace.

It's like we truly are calm inside, despite of what's outside of us.

You are my Side Peace!

We are not our society's description…

We are support; we are what is needed after the storm, we are what's needed before the storm, we are what's needed during the storm…

We are beside each other bringing peace…

PERSPECTIVE

I had two thoughts when I wrote this article. I was thinking about a woman being a man's rib which is located on the side. The side! I was also thinking that we need PEACE by our sides to complete who we are because we are constantly fighting the world. Home should be peaceful, and home is where the heart is. I think we allow our minds to become perverted and redefine positive terms negatively. The label "side piece" is a negative term in the world, but in reality, there is a piece of man that needs to be completed, and that completion needs to come from one woman. His friend, girlfriend, fiancé, and finally wife. She is the final piece bringing peace to him. When men were created, we were created completely alone! Then God made us incomplete and took from us to create woman. If we understand that she is a part of what completes us, we would value her. At the same time, a woman needs to value who she is and what she brings to us, which is completeness. She also needs to find where she fits to complete him.

Men: what does it mean for her to be your rib? Women: what does it mean to be his rib?

TAKE IT PERSONAL

_____

_____

_____

_____

_____

_____

_____

DEAR FUTURE WIFE

Chapter 16

ROLES AND RELATIONSHIPS

Society, roles, and success are changing when it comes to what a relationship looks like between romantic partners. Traditionally, the man is the one leading financially. If we were to look back, society would tell us that the man was the breadwinner and the woman was the homemaker. Before I get into that historically evidenced picture of a relationship between a man and a woman, I want to make it clear that women have always worked and provided financially in addition to contributing to the "homemaker" role. I won't get into details and if you are interested, there are stories, articles, and researched evidence of women making significant contributions to the household financially. Now let's talk about the "Independent Woman."

There is a huge disconnect between the independent woman and today's man. The woman devalues the man's role because men don't deliver "traditions." Men don't possess the ability to lead a woman, be head of the household, be strong enough in their identities and fit the definition of a "man." When in reality, through the woman's journey of self-care, strength development, "get ahead," survival, and "I no longer need a man" ideology, she forgets, or perhaps never learned or desired to know the value of a man. It's not that the man can't lead, be "the man," provide, be strong, have his identity, it's the fact that while she was on her own personal journey, she learned what was best for her. She learned what it took for her to get where she is. She learned how to be strong and she learned that nobody can give her what she wants for her in the way that she wants it given. She learned that nobody can please her the way she pleases her.

She learned that nobody can live up to what she has done for herself. She learned that nobody can treat her how she treats herself. Although this is true and a great understanding of yourself (to the women), it should not be applied to anyone outside of yourself. This is flawed thinking because a man can never be you.

A man comes with the thought of how he was designed to be. He is taught to protect and provide with adjustments. He may not be able to be exactly how you were to yourself but determine if what he can offer you is enough. This is not an excuse for a man to be stagnant or settle in his efforts. He must forever learn new ways to solidify his role. Creativity and effort can easily replace spending/financial posturing. The question is *do you want him or yourself with a beard?* It's hard to address the needs of such woman when she needs to control what support looks like. Women have to make sure they aren't attempting to make a man weaker to maintain their strength because the truth is that a man can match and complement your strength, allowing you to breathe easy. A secure man will never question his ability to lead based on the reactions of his woman. He may change his approach or strategy, but he will never question his manhood. If a man questions his manhood when dating, courting, in a relationship, he needs to empower himself or walk away.

Chapter 17

CAN I LOVE YOU?

Dear Future Wife,

Will you let me?
Can I see who you are?
I can say that!
I can ask that!
I really want that!
But I can't do that without you.
Without you letting me in…
I don't expect it all at "hello," but at least crack the door!
At the same time, I want you to know that I've left an entry ajar for you as well.
Cracked two ways!
Cracked with imperfections willing to be repaired with your desires while remaining imperfect even after your seal.
Sometimes I will stretch, and your seal will stretch to the point where I release my imperfections but don't give up.
Don't give up on our chance.
Cracked with the identical idea that I am not wide open, and it will take time.
I know you read this letter and are planning the final destination, but I need time on the journey.
I want to be your end result, trust me, but it takes a while for my door to open wider.

I write wide open, but life disallows me the width of an ending.
You may ask "why aren't you what you want?"
And my answer is "I am constantly working on it."
I am working with you, watching us, paying attention to, learning, sharing, giving, taking, forgiving, asking for forgiveness and planning together what that "want" will be.
I am not a selfish planner of someone else's life. That isn't fair and rarely works because it hurts to disappoint and be disappointed.
Will you share the journey?
Will you let me?
Can I see who you are?
Can I love you?
Are you love available?
I want to love well enough to forgive the bad.

PERSPECTIVE

As I wrote this, I realized that in order to get to a place of readiness, we need to address our issues, heal from our pasts, renew and restore our minds, bodies, and souls. We need to literally clean out the images and experiences that are holding us hostage. We also need to prepare to pursue or to be pursued, date, court, and marry. This does not mean that we discredit what we've learned; it means that we ask, "What was the lesson (as opposed to the damage)?" Think about the relationship that you remember the most. This is what I call emotional memory. How is that impacting you right now? Is that a relationship you want to repeat in terms of behaviors and experiences?

TAKE IT PERSONAL

_____

_____

_____

_____

_____

_____

_____

_____

_____

DEAR FUTURE WIFE

Chapter 18

THE SEARCH IS OVER

Dear Future Wife,

All the things I thought I wanted were not what I needed.

There is a certain level of discovery that needed to take place inside of me as opposed to looking to outside forces. I no longer want to imagine dating a woman without knowing what I perceive are your deficiencies.

I realized I wanted to take other women's gifts and implant them into you, but the truth is that I chose you for the gifts you have and who you are.

As amazing as I think I am, I know you make me more believable.

When I stand beside you, I feel better, I am better, and I know better.

On the days you are not around, I feel myself shrinking. Finding you was empowering.

Once a man realizes that he has found the woman he was searching for, he has to adjust his thought process as well as his actions.

During my search, parts of me had to die, because the parts that keep me searching are no longer needed. The hunter in me had to retire, because the hunt was over.

I no longer needed to go to the forest where the game is, because I have all I need at home.

I've searched for someone to build with.

Someone to build me up.

Someone I could build up.

Even though it was a rough journey, we are here.

You were working on you when I found you. I was working on me when I found you. We were working.

I realized that much of my search was a distraction from you.
Before finding you, I had all the tools to perform what I thought was a perfect search, but then I realized with each finding, my tools would lose their perfection.

Finally, I realized I needed to lose what I thought was perfection, because I didn't need to be a perfect finder/searcher.
I needed to find you and lose my ability to search.

What good is being a perfect finder when you no longer want to look for more than what's in front of you? Why do I need those skills anymore? You're found. The search is over!

PERSPECTIVE

Proverbs 18:22 states that "he who finds a wife, finds a good thing and obtains favor from the Lord." Notice the singular form. So many times we become experts of pursuit and we try to build a wife from a combination of our experiences and fail to realize that we skip over what we need. We will always be searching if we don't decide to focus and pour into what's right in front of us. Some men have wives at our fingertips, but still reach for more. The truth is she will always lack at something. You will always lack at something but it doesn't mean she is not worth being your one and only. You can always find what you need in her, or help pull it out of her, or even still discover what you need yourself with the skills and abilities she has in other areas. Will you end your search? What will it take?

TAKE IT PERSONAL

_____

_____

_____

_____

_____

_____

_____

_____

_____

DEAR FUTURE WIFE

Chapter 19

WILL YOU SUBMIT?

Dear Future Wife,

What does submission mean to you?
What does it mean to me?
Will you consider submitting to me?
Will you submit to me?
Will you allow me to lead you?
Will you trust you in my hands?
Before you say "no," let me explain.
I plan to submit to you.
I plan to listen and value you.
I plan to learn you with my mind, body, heart, and soul.
I plan to let God guide me in the ways that you deserve.
I believe submission is trusting me.
I understand what you have been through and what you have seen.
But!!!! I am not what you have been through nor what you have seen!!!
I have done the work to get me in the door of consideration.
I have learned to love myself.
I have learned what it takes to love, listen, and lead.
Lead by example.
I have a plan!
My plan takes you into consideration every step of the way.
I plan to value you and submit to you as well.

I come to lead; not rule.
I come to listen, take heed, take your advice, practice my word, choose your choice, humble myself, and honor your entire being.
You are worth what you are designed to be.
I want what seems to be outdated.
I want and will work to obtain what seems to be a fairytale.
I want us to be able to disagree but still value each other.
When you submit to me, it does not take away from who you are.
When you submit to me, it does not take away your accomplishments.
When you submit to me, it highlights the work you have done and the value you have put in how much I mean to you.
I love the fact that you made me earn your submission.
I respect the work you made me do.
I respect the fact that you noticed I worked on me before I could lead you.
I respect your patience that came from a healthy place.
I respect that you understood that the competition didn't exist between us.
We leave our egos at the door.
We leave our egos at hello.
We hold hands to secure our bond and not to control or make sure we know where the other person is.
I understood that it was scary to be vulnerable.
I understand what you are feeling, and I want you to know that if I let you down, I let myself down.
Let's submit to each other.
Here is my control; can I have yours?
Bryson Tiller sings it best, "Give me all of you in exchange for me."
Submission can be defined many ways and I choose to believe it is acceptance and consent.
I accept you and consent to you.
As I am down on one knee, will you accept me and consent to me?
Together, we plan to be equal.

PERSPECTIVE

Often, we see the word "submission" and assume it is only the woman who is supposed to do it. We like to hold on to Ephesians 5:22, "Wives, submit to your own husbands as you do to the Lord." We ignore the verse right before it that reads, "Submit to one another out of reverence for Christ." Even those who don't follow the Bible quote Ephesians 5:22. Submission isn't an opportunity to control another person; it's an opportunity to serve the other person, care for, protect, give to, and sacrifice with compromise.

Men: we have to be willing to be someone a woman is willing to submit to and know that once she does, we can and will protect her choice. There is nothing like a two-way street. Imagine a woman who trusts you with her life and livelihood. What will it take for you to submit? What does equal submission look like?

TAKE IT PERSONAL

_____

_____

_____

_____

_____

_____

_____

_____

DEAR FUTURE WIFE

Chapter 20

YOUR BEAUTY IS SPECIFIC

Dear Future Wife,

It has nothing to do with society.
It has nothing to do with comparison.
It has nothing to do with anyone else.
Your beauty is specific to you.
I have never connected with someone who looked so gorgeous in the essence
of being who she is.
Your beauty said "hello" before I heard your voice.
I stared at you and the greeting played out.
I grabbed you mentally and you held on.
We realized that the prayers we prayed were for each other and a spiritual
confirmation became evident.
I promise I have never seen someone so beautiful in my life.
I am flawed but know that my flaws were covered by who you are, how you
are, and what you are.
You had this look of "why me?"
And I didn't understand "why not you?"
Your smile was evident through your eyes when you tried to conceal or save
face.
I don't want you to coach yourself out of showing how intentionally beautiful
you are.
Will you allow me to be in awe and just receive it?

Will you allow my attention to your details to be sufficient enough?

I'm asking because I don't think you need another man's attention to fill a void.

If you ever get to that point, let's talk about it.

Let me know until I get it right.

If it's deeper than me, let's continue to talk about it and work together until you know I'm here and all you need.

Your beauty is deeper than a vision through the eyes.

It's a holistic vision.

You're beautiful when you smile, pray, talk, cry, share, care, sleep, forgive, are upset, say no, stand firm, pray again, love, allow yourself to be loved, accomplish, fail, pose, posture, say "I do," commit, be faithful, and work together.

PERSPECTIVE

We live in a world of comparison and distractions. We log on and see all types of women and beauty. We also see some people trying to look like others and not embracing their own beauty.

As men, we have to choose her and compliment her beauty. We can't be distracted by the access that we have to others. It is a slippery slope because it's not that another woman is more beautiful than the one you have; all beauty is different. Think of the things that distract you and how you manage them. Delete them, unfollow them, all while protecting the beauty beside you. What do you need to change?

TAKE IT PERSONAL

_____

_____

_____

_____

_____

_____

_____

_____

_____

Dear Future Wife

Chapter 21

FIVE LOVE LANGUAGES

Dear Future Wife,

In order for me to really understand how to love you, I decided to pay attention to how your love communicates.
You have five different ways you speak lovingly.
I want to learn how to understand every word your heart speaks.
I just ask that you speak clearly.
Speak from the heart of love and not of protection.
Be honest so that when I speak back, I am loving you in a language you can agree with.

Let's communicate:

Words of Affirmation

I will compliment you on who you are while building you up. I will make sure to wake you up with a praise of how beautiful you are. I will make sure I tell you "goodnight" with the goal of initiating your dreams of us forever. These words will be natural and genuine without a goal of gaining anything selfishly. I am making sure I influence your happiness. Random I miss you, an unsolicited I love you, a thought of you followed up by, "You are beautiful."

I know how sensitive you are to my words, and I don't want to create insecurity or tear you down in any way. I want to speak life and not influence the death of who you are. Because of our love and my role, I will feed you affirming words. I will speak to your heart!

Quality Time

No cell phone, no social media, no television, no radio, no distractions, nothing but you. I will leave everything outside of you in a cloud and walk away so that it's clear to you that I am focused on you. It's your time and nothing else can take away from what you deserve. You remain scheduled in my daily calendar and I titled it "Her." This way the time is yours, the location is "where you are," the reason is you, the focus is your heart, and I will make quality time my priority.

I won't put off the time with you. No rescheduling my love for you. I will make sure that I am available.

Acts of Service

Relax, I got it. Let me open the door for you. I will make you dinner and do the dishes. Put your feet up and know that I will take care of everything to your liking. I will wash your car and put gas in it. What do you need from the store? The DVR is set to play your favorite television show. I made coffee; the book you're reading is waiting for you, and the room temperature is set to your preference. I brought you a bottle of your favorite wine, started your bath and lit some candles. Your robe is hanging, only to be put on after I dry you off.

Receiving Gifts

My gifts to you will make sense and be purposeful. Think about the things you wanted or needed. Not just shoes or a purse but the gift of effort and consistency. While in the store, I will say to myself, "*Dear Future Wife* likes that," and I will pick it up. Gifts to remind you that I care for you and I am thinking about you. A card for you to read with my words on them.

Physical Touch

Let me have your hand as we walk. Let our fingers lock as we talk. Good morning hug with a kiss on the forehead to say, "Have a good day." A shoulder massage. Rubbing your arm. Lay on my chest while I wrap my arm across yours. I need your hand again as I lead you to the bedroom...

PERSPECTIVE

Knowing her love language is important. Knowing what she likes is key to your happiness. It's rewarding to pay close attention to her happiness. It's amazing what happens when we do. We are skilled to cater to each love language. Also, it is imperative to take it seriously for ourselves. Understand what you need and want and be honest and open about it with yourself first. What's your love language and what is your partner's? What can you do differently to protect you both?

TAKE IT PERSONAL

_____

_____

_____

_____

_____

_____

_____

_____

_____

_____

Chapter 22

SUGA MAMA

Dear Future Wife,

Now that I have your attention...
It's not what you think; I don't want your money.
I don't want an enabler.
I don't want you to replace my mother's role in my life.
I just want the mentality of a Sugar Mama!
Imagine the thought process of a sugar mama, now take away the money.
I want that type of support.
I want to experience your genuine interest in me and my dreams.
I don't want to live off of you.
I appreciate the fact that you wouldn't allow it.
Don't give blindly.
I will not let you do all the work!
That isn't the vision of what a man, provider, or husband looks like.
This has zero to do with dependency on you doing everything while I figure out what I want to do with my life.
I will not approach you without my plan in motion and ability to be self-sufficient.
I will not pursue you without my vision.
I will not look at you as a meal ticket.
I am not a mama's boy looking to be supported by a woman.
I acknowledge that you have that ability but that isn't my draw to you.

I applaud everything that you have accomplished.

I applaud your success.

I applaud your ability to be financially independent as a direct result of your hard work.

I am not looking to live off of that hard work and you shouldn't let me.

With that being said, I am a MAN and I still need/want your sugar, Mama.

I still want your support.

I want the concept of a sugar mama, but without money.

I want you to support me emotionally.

Before I ask you to respect me, I will give you something to respect.

I will respect you as well.

I may need you to just rub my back in silence.

I may need you to lay on my shoulder to let me know you're here.

I may need you to put your head on my lap to reassure me that you will be here.

I need you to be my biggest fan.

I desire the push from my woman.

I watched other women cheer on their men and I want that!

Sometimes I may need encouragement from you with phrases like ,"You got this babe."

I can push myself, but it feels much better when I hear you say, "You can do it."

I love hearing, "You have done it before so there isn't anything to be afraid of."

Your confidence in me is the sugar I need.

I am not afraid of your honest feedback, give me sugar.

Being my biggest fan shows that you really love me and want what is best for us, give me sugar.

With that being said, don't let me be unrealistic, give me sugar.

Correct me when you know the dream isn't something I should be pursuing, give me sugar.

If I am still trying to rap at thirty plus; if I am focused on being an entrepreneur, but unwilling to put in the work, and if I am unwilling to work somewhere else while pursuing my dream, hold me accountable.

Correct me if I am going overboard on everything.

Support looks like encouraging sustainability for myself.
Let me break some of it down.
I want kisses.
I want hugs.
I want that sugar.
I want you to support my realistic plans, dreams, and visions.
I want you to challenge me to explain my plans, dreams, and visions.
I want you to have my back the same way you want me to have yours.
I want the sweetness only you can bring.
I want to hear the sweetness of your voice at home when I have just taken
on the world.
I want to see the sweetness in your smile.
I want to be the reason you smile.
This is the sugar I am looking for.
Will you give me some sugar?

PERSPECTIVE

The emotional and mental sugar mama is what we really need. When the money is put aside, and she believes in you, that is the most empowering position a woman can occupy. What do you need from your future or current wife to feel like you have the best gift ever? What do you need or want from a woman to feel and know that God blessed you with her?

Women: what makes you that ideal sugar mama?

TAKE IT PERSONAL

_____

_____

_____

_____

_____

_____

_____

_____

_____

_____

Chapter 23

SECURING YOUR INSECURITIES

Dear Future Wife,

I realized that even though I wish I could create your confidence, I don't have the ability to do so.

I recognize the areas where you don't give yourself enough credit.

I will make my goal to feed your strengths in hopes of helping you realize how great you are.

I want to endorse the moments when you smile in recognition of your greatness.

I understand it has been tough to enjoy who you are based on how you were failed.

I desire to be a major part of the reason you succeed.

Succeed in love, life, and being who you are designed to be.

I need your help.

I need you to let me in.

I promise my goal is for us to win.

Winning is us making our dreams of love come true.

The *Knight in Shining Armor* you dreamed about will be me.

The Queen I proposed to will manifest as you.

You have been hurt before and let down by my fellow man.

You have been told a story that remained in that state of words.

Words that weren't fact because they were told to you by a fictional character.

Tell me what your insecurities are so I can wrap them in my secure arms in hopes to transform them into the opposite of what you expected from a man.

My understanding of this is clear based on my personal experiences.

I have never been perfect, but I want to learn how to perfectly secure you in that vision I have of us.

That means me making you able to breathe, walk, and believe in what you dream love feels like.

I want you to know that when I don't answer my phone; I'm not ignoring you.

I want you to know that when I am meeting with a female friend, she is your friend, and if she isn't, she isn't allowed in our circle.

I want you to know that when a person in my history attempts to resurface that their efforts will be in vain.

I want you to know that my words of promise to you are dependable.

I want you to know that when I am with my fellas, the goal is to get home to love and not to succumb to adulterous lust.

I want you to know that my thoughts are always with you and I want to strengthen our vows.

I want you to know that I live in fear of messing up my forever.

I want you to know that I will never compare your beauty to another woman.

I want you to know that my compliments are genuine and not for gain.

I want you to know that you do not have to be perfect!

I want you to know that sex isn't better than love.

I want you to know that the password on my phone is not there to keep secrets from you.

I want you to know that I need you to know we are exclusive for and to each other.

I want you to know that I have insecurities too and you are helping me get over them.

I want you to know that I will express my fears to you and desire the same with hopes of us nurturing each other.

When there are two people on my shoulders influencing my decisions in this relationship, you are the angel on the right.

Securing Your Insecurities

I will strive to make the right decisions.
Your insecurities are my priorities to secure.
I will love you out of those insecurities.
I won't allow insecurities to define who you are; they will be who you *were*.
Our success story will be described with a smile that says, "I trust you."

PERSPECTIVE

We all have insecurities in some area of our lives, and as men, it is up to us to make sure our behaviors secure our wives. Even if we see the insecurities, there are things we can do to protect them. We should not be contributing to those insecurities. There *are* extreme cases (of insecure women) but even in those, our responsibility is not to make it worse. We are protectors. Insecurities should never be an excuse to do anything damaging to your relationship. What do you need in order to manage your insecurities and protect hers?

TAKE IT PERSONAL

_____

_____

_____

_____

_____

_____

_____

_____

_____

Chapter 24

WHY A WIFE ALWAYS COMES FIRST

There was a social media meme that sparked a debate. The meme has a visual representation of four individuals and poses the question, "Who Comes First?" The four individuals are of a mother, wife, daughter, and baby mother.

Immediately I thought to myself, "Why are we describing the mother of the child as a baby mother?" That's derogatory and demeaning. Let's change the narrative and give respect to all parties involved.

We have to lead! She is the mother of your child. Now that I have made that clear, I thought the decision for everyone was a no-brainer.

Wife, right?

Or so I thought. I found myself in many different debates explaining why I believe the wife is always first. I was astounded at the thought process and reasoning of why others chose other options as first. With that being said, let's discuss each role, and I'll present my reasoning of why the wife should come first.

Mother

We love our mothers and they are amazing! They birthed us and nurtured us to the best of their abilities. They helped us grow into the men we are today.

They are very knowledgeable and have played the roles of wife, mother, and child at one time in their lives. They can offer some great insight on who should be first out of the four. This may be based on bias for themselves, the child, wife, or child's mother.

As great as mom has been to us, she is not first, nor second, and sometimes she will be a toss-up between third and last. Moms are a reference and not the source. Their roles decreased immensely once we became men.

We can no longer lay on their laps or their bosoms and depend on them to take care of us. We become men of our own homes and start our own families.

No matter how awesome mothers are, we can no longer depend on them to save us! We are no longer the men of their homes nor should we treat them as our spouses.

Giving them the power to lead us will hinder our relationships. This does not mean their advice isn't invaluable; it means we should absorb their knowledge and apply it appropriately ensuring it doesn't put us in a boy's role.

We are men and the head of our new families!

Mother of our Children

This section may be short because their opinions on a man's marriage begins and ends with the children. They will not have an influence on decisions that don't impact the children directly. Don't let them influence your husband and wife relationships.

It is up to the husband to control the relationship between mother, wife, and child's mother.

Make sure there are clear boundaries.

The husband must also facilitate the relationship between the child and the child's mother to make sure all parties are comfortable.

YES, we have a lot of responsibility, we created the environment, so we must manage it. We must not allow the mothers of our children to control the relationships between our mutual children and our wives. Manage it!

I get it, our children don't have to accept our wives as their new mothers, BUT the children must respect them as adults and as our WIVES!

Child

They are first before you get married. If you think you have always put your child first, think about the times you sought a babysitter or switched the schedule with your child's mother to go out on a date with your wife, who was at the time your girlfriend.

Got it?!

I have read women say, "I would never expect a man to put me in front of his child."

That is good because it isn't up to you, it is up to the man.

We, as men, need to balance the relationships. We as men, need to show our children how highly we respect and think of our wives.

As a father, it is up to me to show my son how he should treasure his future wife. If I had a daughter, it would be up to me to provide an example of how she should be treated as a wife. This does not mean the child will be neglected in any way, this shows order.

Children will receive love and understand relationship transition. They invite additional love from others.

It is up to us as men to marry women that we are confident will be additional parents and extensions of us. We can't allow children to cause rifts by splitting us up. We must be on one accord with our wives to show them that we are a team and will take care of them. We have to teach them roles.

The children don't make decisions in your household!

Wife

Happy wife, happy life! Thou shall not neglect the wife in any area.

Should I stop there?!

If you have read the other categories, they all show why and where we need to put our wives first. In parenting, we need to have a partnership. When we get married, it will be our responsibility to lead and show our children an example of how a husband is supposed to love his wife and lead his family. Our wives need and should be secure in our relationships.

She is the queen of the household. Relationships with mothers and mothers of our children are outside of our household.

You and your wife are a united front. Make decisions together. Complete actions together. Your love and respect will be an example to everyone.

Your relationship with your wife is the most important relationship to maintain. Your child will be fine! When you chose your wife, you considered the relationship she would have with your child.

When you chose your wife, you considered the role you would play in managing the relationship between your wife and the mother of your child. When you chose your wife, you considered how you would manage the relationship between your wife and your mother.

Keep home happy by keeping your queen happy!

Chapter 25

YOU MADE IT SAFE

Dear Future Wife,

A man needs to feel safe in order to move forward in a relationship.

I realized I needed safety in my relationship and you made that happen.

You created a bubble that protects any and everything I ever desired to share with anyone.

I found safety in who you were as opposed to who you were trying to be for me.

That safety made me gravitate towards you.

The word "potential" was considered dangerous until we met and examined our potential specifically and purposefully.

I saw you for who you were and didn't think about prior to that moment in your life. I decided I could love you there.

I saw the potential in us spending the rest of our lives together.

Everything else was a bonus.

I appreciate you doing the same thing for me. You didn't want to marry what I could be; you married who I am.

You didn't plan to change me into your ideal man or try to mold me into the husband of your dreams.

You said, "I choose who you are today to spend my FOREVER tomorrow with."

There were a couple of traits I saw in you that showed me it was safe for me to move forward.

I paid attention to how you treated others and although they received great treatment, I naturally received your best.

I began to experience what my friends were getting from their wives and thought "this is what they are talking about…"

You made life bigger than yourself. You were selfless, put others first, and went the extra mile to keep everyone happy.

You created this bubble of selflessness and anyone who stepped in it benefited without you expecting returned favors.

You knew how to balance this because you didn't allow yourself to be used or burned out.

You showed me how to do the same, just by being you.

You put God before everything.

Dear Future Wife,

You made it safe to say and show I trust you. I trust you with all my insecurities. You know everything about me. You were there for the worst of times and best of times.

Your loyalty made me realize it is okay to let down my guard and let you in. I watched you love and express passion. That strength broke through my safety armor, because it showed me how you love.

You gave me evidence of your wealth of love and I wanted in on that experience. I wanted to combine loves.

We created "Wealthy Love."

You made it safe for me to abandon my ego and bravado when it came to you.

The consistency in your words made it safe.

There is safety in who you are!

You made it safe for me to say, "I'm struggling," because your response didn't make it worse. You reminded me that I wasn't alone.

You made it safe for me to say I need help. You reminded me that you were there.

You made it safe for me to say "that" wasn't my expertise.

You made it safe for me to be honest.

You made it safe for me to say that I'm falling out of love because you knew

I wanted to regain our balance and stand tall.

Your, "How are you?" wasn't generic and routine. It was specific to what we discussed. It was specific to an area where I was struggling. It was specific to an area where I was succeeding.

Your words were intentional.

I know if I wanted to have a career or job change you would be there to talk it through with me.

I knew that our disagreements were safe with us.

I knew that my biggest fears were never going to be played on or displayed.

I knew our conversations wouldn't travel.

Your help wasn't conditional or based off of self-serving contingencies.

You genuinely wanted others to succeed and I experienced that first hand.

You didn't try to control me; you only controlled what you accepted from me.

I appreciated the difference.

You made "home" safe, and home is wherever *we* are.

PERSPECTIVE

This is one of the most important articles I have written. It was so important that I felt the need to interview some important people who are experienced in this topic for their insights. Thank you, Daryl Towe, Tyson Bates, Taurus Hinton, and Jeffrey Whitehorn.

Sometimes we see "safe" as a bad thing. We align safe with settling. Think about it for a second. Who doesn't want to feel safe in a relationship? Why not pour into a relationship that is safe for you to be free in love? What do you need from your significant other to feel safe? What do you need to provide your significant other for him or her to be safe?

TAKE IT PERSONAL

_____

_____

_____

_____

_____

_____

_____

_____

_____

Chapter 26

CAN WE COMMUNICATE?

Dear Future Wife,

Can we listen to each other with an open ear?
I am asking because I don't want either of us to prepare to respond while the other is expressing ourselves.
I want to practice hungry listening where what I learn about you feeds me and the relationship. I want us to be receptive. I want us to encourage more. How big is your appetite for learning me?
Can we make it a goal to be quiet until the other finishes?
I know this is hard sometimes when we want to interject because we feel our point is more valid. Cutting someone off tells the other person, "Your opinion isn't important or valid." It screams selfishness.
I am going to be honest, I don't want to verbally compete. I will shut down and let you have your words. I will just agree. I can imagine that you will do the same thing. Where will that leave us? Unheard, frustrated and without resolution.
Can we pay attention to body language?
Part of listening is noticing how things are affecting the other. If I see you cross your arms, roll your eyes, give me the face that says, 'I'm losing you,' I will try to bring you back in.
If you see me turn my head, close my eyes, deep sigh, or anything specific to me, try to bring me back in.

We can also pay attention to what is not going over well and change the approach.

Show me what you look like when you're upset, hurt, over it and finished. Let's discuss what that looks like.

Can we watch our tones?

I understand things may be frustrating, but we can talk to each other instead of yelling or speaking with an aggressive tone.

If either of us need to take a break, allow the other one to do so. Let's not abuse the timeout to avoid having the discussion. I'm not going anywhere; I will be patient, because I want to figure this out. I hope you are the same way.

If I sound condescending, let me know; I will apologize, and work to change my tone.

If you start to talk in a "matter of fact" way, allow me to point it out and let's start again. I understand we are not robots or without emotion; I just believe we can get a point across without yelling, screaming, or shouting.

Can we look at each other while talking?

I want to stay connected and look at you with intent. Intent to love you through eyes of sincerity. If I look away, I am either disappointed in myself, you, or us.

I may be upset. I may be hurt. Get back in my sight by gently turning my chin to say, "I'm here, it's okay. Stay with me."

If you turn away, allow me to gently turn your head back towards me while conveying, "It's okay. Stay with me. I'm here."

If touching isn't your thing at that moment, tell me how to reel you back in. I love to show my respect for what you have to say, and I hope you do as well.

I am locked in, besides who can stay mad at your beauty for a long period of time?

Can we be honest?

Honesty is not just truthfulness; it is also being direct and not leaving anything out.

As hard as it is to do; let's not keep secrets.

I truly believe that dishonesty, lack of openness, and dancing around an issue creates a "roommates with a ring" environment. Imagine the burden we would have to carry. It would destroy us.

If we can't accept each other for who we are, where we have been, or our intentions then we have some serious things to consider.

Can I say I don't like something?

Will you tell me what doesn't work for you?

Can we communicate in silence?

We say so much in silence. The conversations of a hug. The words of a look. The statements of a kiss. I hear our future as an infinite symbol. Holding hands.

I hope you accept my responses.

P.S. - Can we keep "us" in-house? If we need help, let's see an unbiased professional.

PERSPECTIVE

Communication is key to a healthy relationship. How have you struggled to communicate? Men sometimes struggle to express ourselves in a healthy way. Partners need to practice active listening, patience, tone appropriateness, and being careful with words. We need to keep talking about our feelings. We need to pay attention to our body language when speaking and listening to each other. There is a such thing as communicating in silence; we have to stop avoiding and assuming. I know that some of us men have never been taught or learned how to communicate, but now is the perfect time to trust your voice with her. We have to exercise clear communication, which means asking for clarity when we are uncertain. Say what you mean and work hard to say it in a way you want it to be received. We have to practice control by taking emotions out of it. Take a second to practice what you want to say. We should also be constructive with our communication because the tongue has the power of life or death. Ask yourself if what you're saying will bring life or death to the relationship. How can you improve communication? How has it impacted your previous relationships? How would you like your communication to be in your current or future relationship?

TAKE IT PERSONAL

_____

_____

_____

_____

_____

_____

_____

Chapter 27

AM I ENOUGH?

Dear Future Wife,

This is all I have. This is what I promise to give. Is this enough?

We may not see a complete change in the other immediately, but we can celebrate our selfless adjustments for each other.

I have a heart that is forever evolving but committed to you.

Is it enough that I will try my hardest, but may not always be exactly what you need?

Is it enough that what I offer made you smile on Monday, but may annoy you by Saturday?

Is it enough that my shortcomings may be greater than my attributes?

Is it enough that I won't be perfect in most situations, but I will be present in every way that I can?

Is it too much to ask for you to communicate your needs and not have me guess or expect me to always know?

Is it too much that some days I just don't have the strength?

Is it too much for me to come to you for help while struggling to express it?

Is it too much for us to figure this out together?

Is it enough that I may not be as financially stable as your coworkers, friend's man, male family member, or other men you may know or see?

Is it too much to ask that we establish our own pace as opposed to trying to keep up with what is happening around us? This doesn't mean that I will drag you along; it just means our pressure comes from our personal love as opposed to outside pushes and influences.

Is it too much that consistency doesn't mean perfection? I think sometimes we confuse consistency with always. As in always make you feel the same way by being the same emotional presence. The same psychological presence where you always feel like I am exactly what you want at the time.

Is it enough that I may not always be exactly what you want, but I'll always be what you need: stable and present?

Is it enough that I can talk and at the same time not respond like your coworker or other male friend?

Am I enough to share your struggles with, while discussing your fears, even though you know my flaws and limitations?

Is giving what I can, which may not always be what you want, okay?

PERSPECTIVE

Vulnerability isn't always about telling your significant other that you need him/her when you are struggling. Those are simply vulnerable moments connected to a need. Full vulnerability is telling your significant other that you may not always be able to give what he or she needs, but you will give all you have. This allows you to acknowledge your effort and shortcomings. This allows your partner to decide whether you are enough for him or her. Vulnerability is the ability to admit that you can't fulfill every need no matter how hard you try. Ask yourself and your relationship partner if you are enough based on his or her needs, not what the outside world projects. What does vulnerability mean to you? Is it scary? Why?

TAKE IT PERSONAL

DEAR FUTURE WIFE

Chapter 28

WHAT NURTURING A MAN LOOKS LIKE

Yes, you are about to read another message by a man who has written a "how to" that is directed towards women. The difference is that this message is intended to be a reference for women and something that men should thoroughly review and soak in.

As a man, you should first ask yourself "what does 'nurture' mean?" As a woman, try to intellectually emotionalize the term "nurture" in relation to a man. Nurturing does not mean you are dealing with an overly sensitive man who needs to be coddled. This is a description of the way "nurturing" fits a man's needs long term.

Let's be honest – sometimes, he doesn't know what he needs. Sometimes he doesn't value what a woman's presence does for his life. Sometimes she doesn't know what he needs. Sometimes she doesn't know her value and assumes he is "just another male with a generalized list of desires from a woman."

Keep these important points in mind when nurturing a man. A man needs to understand himself and what he wants in and out of life. He can't expect a woman to match or complement him when he is all over the place. Until he is sure of these things, she will never be the right one for him and he will never know what's right for him. He will qualify a woman temporarily and then subconsciously put her on another trial run. She will win small battles but will always be behind in the war. "War" may be a bad term, but it is a war – a battle that he is having within himself and she is trying to fight alongside him without knowing who she is fighting. This can lead to her becoming an adversary as opposed to the ally she is trying to be.

How can a man attract a like-minded woman when his thoughts, emotions, purpose, and focus are scattered? We have to get clear about those things and organize them in our heads and hearts to allow them to influence our attraction to partnerships.

This isn't about being able to physically nurture a man with sex. Referring back to my previous comment, I want to emphasize a point – a woman who doesn't know you can make you feel good, man. But a woman who knows you can make you a great man. She can please you in ways that nobody can. This is nurturing. I guess I could give the "definition" right here: care for and encourage the growth and development of...

This segues into the purpose of this chapter, which is to provide men with a guide and women a reference on what it looks like for a man to be nurtured. This isn't a solo opinionated position. I asked a few of my single, dating, courting, committed, married, and divorced male friends for their descriptions of what it felt/feels like to be nurtured by a woman. I chose them because I trust them. I chose them because they have a clear direction. I chose them because their experiences have shaped their presence and present.

What we discovered was this: nurturing a man is standing beside him in his purpose. It is assuring him that he is on the right path and making sure he is on the right path once it's chosen. That may sound confusing, but the key is that it's up to the man to be direct. MEN, WE HAVE TO BE DIRECT. Nurturing is being that second leg to balance his gift, goal, and finish line. If his passion is clear, nurturing is easy. Nurturing looks like reassurance. Nurturing is the sunlight on your man's darkest day. Nurturing is hearing "you have me" when the world takes everything from him. Nurturing is sometimes quiet, but says, "I got you" by you just being there. The definition of "being there" is specific to that man you are being specific to. Here are some examples:

Terrence Foster says, "Nurturing is knowing the right things to say regardless of the moment. When upset, her not being silent because she is at a loss for words from not knowing what to say. Sometimes doing things without having to tell her, not having to think, basically knowing him and what his needs are at the time. At times, knowing him better than he does."

Taurus Hinton says, "Nurturing is constantly encouraging growth, never allowing me to settle, or become complacent… reminds me that she follows my lead. Above all, I know that she has my back."

Daryl from Team Towe (Husband and Wife), "She is two steps ahead of me with my needs and nine times out of ten has already completed them. If not, she is in motion to complete them. For example, in business, if I'm overloaded with work or mentally burnt out and she notices it. She will take on some of the tasks… pull out a blanket– lay me on the couch and encourage me to relax my body, mind, and soul to recharge. She reassures me. She is always thoughtful towards my family, going the extra mile with communicating with them. Whether it is holidays, birthdays, random calls etc., she knows how important family is to me."

Jeff Whitehorn says, "I like simplicity, she fixes my plate when she doesn't have to because she wants me to know that she appreciates/acknowledges that I take care of her, too. She goes out of her way to leave messages on the fridge that make a potentially rough day start off positive. I know my beginning."

Tony Jefferson, Jr. says, "Speak life into him. Calm his heart and mind when the world is coming for him. Challenge him to be the best version of himself. Be the best version of herself because whatever they are doing, they are representing each other. Knows his love language."

Nurturing is specific. Nurturing cultivates. Nurturing makes sure. Nurturing is what she is when you let her be. Nurturing is who you are when you are specific.
Be present.
Wrap each other in love.
Be peace to each other.
Create, obtain, and sustain love.
Have the direction you are going, and she will be the light to guide you.

Dear Future Wife

Chapter 29

YOUR WORDS

Dear Future Wife,

I wish you knew the power in your words.

Not in the, "Girl, I let him have it" sense. Instead, I mean the, "I can have what I want through him by the words I speak into him," sense.

A woman's voice carries a man's soul. I can hear it. When you say what you say, I feel the strength that God put in my ears. I am listening.

I wait to hear that you believe [in me and us], your doubts, if you can't support, and the way I should go… all in one conversation.

That may not be realistic, but it shows that I am hanging on to your words.

I pray you choose your next words wisely. I pray you remember what you said before.

Your words are so instrumental in my walk that each step is influenced by what I just heard. What did you say?

Was it a deposit or withdrawal? I want to continue to empower you. I want to continue to hear what you have to say.

What you say means so much to me.

Your words can empower or destroy my day.

That is how much your voice means to me.

Now don't get me wrong, I know I play a role in the content, but you have full control of the context.

I am not expecting perfection; I just pray for protection.

I will protect you, too.

I will speak into you the things you need to hear.

I will also speak of you the way your name deserves.

I often used to hear women tear down their men in private and in public and wonder why there was a disconnect.

I used to hear women tear down their families, friends, associates, coworkers, and strangers, and I wondered if they talked to or about their men the same way.

I don't want that for us.

I am very careful with listening to what you have to say and also how you have to say the things that you say.

I am not a spy.

I am not judging you.

I just want to hear your voice.

I want to make sure you speak life and not death.

We both know the bible says there is life and death in the power of the tongue.

I believe it and I receive it.

I also want to make sure we speak life, power, sustainability, forgiveness, growth, love, respect, adjustment, compromise, submission to each other, and faith into our relationship.

I love your voice and I breathe your words.

PERSPECTIVE

We have an opportunity in relationships to really influence the thought process, emotions, and psyche of our significant others by what, why, and how we speak to them. Think of times when you shouldn't have said something. How did it impact your relationship? Words create feeling which impact action. It won't always be perfect, but we must always be mindful. Take some time to think about where you want to improve. Also, take some time to reflect on where you learned to speak to your significant other. If you are in a relationship, think about what you may have said that hurt your significant other or what did he or she say to hurt you? Address it with an apology and a promise to work on it. Relationships can survive arguments, but they can't survive the threats of leaving. Choose your words carefully.

TAKE IT PERSONAL

_____

_____

_____

_____

_____

_____

_____

_____

DEAR FUTURE WIFE

Chapter 30

I Realize what "Value" Means

Dear Future Wife,

There was a time when I thought value was in experiencing other women.
See I was taught by my peers that conquering increased my value.
At times, I thought that I was not valuable because I couldn't keep up with them.
Each time a woman said "no," I lost worth.
The moment a woman who was deemed as "easy" told me she wanted to "wait," I felt like I wasn't as special as she described... as special as all the other men who came before me yet didn't have to wait.
I looked at her wait as an excuse or rejection as opposed to what I later learned as God's protection.
My mind was all messed up because nobody described the value in the wait; emphasis had always been put on volume.
How could I tell my boys she said "no" when they had received a "yes?"
I did not know my value.
I did not know that her no meant I was worth more than the moment I was trying to experience.
I did not know she didn't know her value, and meanwhile, I was trying to decrease it to an experience, a moment.
As I got older, I realized that some women valued the control of that sexual experience as opposed to valuing the experiences or the men who provided them.

Even when they said they had a ninety-day waiting period, I learned the prize was the sex and not the person.

I've heard that some women would say, "You have to put in work to get this." Therefore, the so-called work was a formality and once men received what they worked for, they valued completing the job and not obtaining the woman.

Although I never experienced that and never had that goal, I have heard about it time and time again.

I used to put value in the dollar and what I could afford, and I used to spend more than I made to be deemed valuable.

After a significant number of overdrafts, I realized my value wasn't tied to expensive items, but was determined by experience.

Spending was exciting so that she could tell her friends, but creating memories was connected to her heart.

The money went, but the effort left residue; it left a stain that wasn't comparable.

I found my value; well so I thought.

I thought because I was exclusive to whoever I dated, I was somehow more valuable, but sometimes that exclusivity was the only focus as opposed to focusing on the actual connection to the person.

I remember creating an experience, and the person I was with missed the value in it, because the financial value wasn't in line to what she was expecting to be "spent on."

I asked myself, "What is value?"

As a man, I realized my value could not be measured or determined by outside forces.

I am valuable, and my values are connected to how I treat you and whether I allow myself to see your value.

Dear Future Wife, you're so valuable and I choose you to increase, save, deposit, invest, withdraw, and match.

I Realize what "Value" Means

Perspective

We put value in the wrong things. We think conquering and control means value when in fact value comes without outside influence. I hope this particular reading and discussion challenges your thought process about what is valued and valuable to you. As the man, what creates value in you? As a woman, what determines your value before you meet him? In and out of the relationship we have to decide what value in us means as opposed to what we think empowers or cures our insecurities and comparison spirits.

Take some time to think about what you try to cover up and how you define value in a person. If it is linked to money, think about the wealthy who experience hurt. Often in a society who values money above all else, we tend to diminish the feelings and emotions of the wealthy as if they have no reason to feel the way they do. What is value to you?

Take it Personal

_____

_____

_____

_____

_____

_____

_____

_____

DEAR FUTURE WIFE

Chapter 31

LOVE-SEX

Dear Future Wife,

I love sex, but I want the love-sex.
There is an art to pleasing, simply, when there is only one to concentrate on.
My desire to please has become bigger than the unsure moments.
In addition to loving sex, I am seeking that love-sex.
I want us to redefine our love life.
I am no longer interested in that "who is next sex."
Be the period to my present sex life.
I am interested in that covenant sex, promise sex, that look in your eyes and see our forever sex.
Covenant sex is where we pledge, promise, agree, commit, and we are forever engaging under our life contract.
Life contract of understanding, willing to work and establish that we are done in our search.
I want that waking up to my wife sex.
I want that wake up in the morning, we respect us sex.
Without the thought of either of us wanting to leave nor wanting the other to leave so we can have our bed back, sex.
I don't want that "another notch on my belt sex," that "check the box sex," nor that "get it out of my system sex."
I don't want you to have that "what have I done sex" nor that "he doesn't count sex."

I want that connection of hearts, making love, sex.

Whether it is play sex, where it's fun that starts from a flirt and a smile.

Whether it's rough, where we need to prove a point or just need to release some aggression.

We will not be predictable, we will be experimental in finding new ways to make our sexual experiences refreshing.

I want to hear, "I didn't know you had that in you."

I want that high-five in the morning when thinking about last night sex.

I want us to be away from each other, have a flashback and plan to repeat sex.

When we get dirty, remember you are my wife. I am your husband and the shower is a few steps away, if needed.

When we argue, we focus on resolving and reward each other with makeup sex.

Nights of passionate sex, where we get that look or a mood and we are reminded of the reason why we said "I do" sex.

I want love-sex.

Sometimes we won't have a lot of time but need it (quickie sex).

I could go into ten more different ways, we will keep ourselves entertained, satisfied, and completed sexually fulfilled like a marathon, wake you up, angry, lazy, but the most important thing is that you are THE ONE, THE ONLY, AND THE LAST.

You gave me all of you in exchange for all of me.

Sex is a responsibility. Sex is a covenant. Sex is a promise. Sex is a permanent connection.

The Netflix account is in our name, so we can chill and watch the movie in its entirety either now or another time.

My goal is to be your "perfect for me, sex."

I will learn your body, mind, soul, and spirit.

We will make love before our bodies touch.

Give me all of you in exchange for me.

Dear Future Wife, love-sex.

PERSPECTIVE

Too many times we rely on sex to be the connection or we use it to sustain a relationship. We think sex means love. We feel that sex is an emotional payment for loyalty and love when sex should be the cherry on top of a loving nurturing relationship. Choosing to love and to build that up before sex means that we wait on the physical penetration until we solidify emotional, psychological, and spiritual connections! If you're a virgin waiting for marriage, be encouraged and don't think you have to give in to fit in. If you're not a virgin and decide to wait, be strong in your decision and know why you're doing it. If you choose to have sex, know and understand the difference between love and sex. Loving sex is different than loving the one you are having sex with. Soul ties are real and no they aren't always tied to sex, but we must be cognizant of what connection is made when sex is made between two people. Ask yourself how has sex tainted your idea of love? How has sex clouded things or made the relationship last longer than it should have been? What does sex mean to you?

TAKE IT PERSONAL

_____

_____

_____

_____

_____

_____

_____

DEAR FUTURE WIFE

Chapter 32

DEAR FUTURE WIFE: SPECIFICALLY

My life changed when my thought process changed.
Once I realized who you were, how you were, what you were, and why you were, my life changed.
How I saw, approached, appreciated, and valued you changed.
I read and understood that you were made specifically for me.
I was here first and had the idea that because I was first, you were secondary.
I thought you were expendable and an option because I was here first.
First wasn't enough because first couldn't make it alone.
I didn't value you the way you deserved before I understood.
You were under me in stature.
Your strength was beneath me.
Your presence was an add-on.
Then it was revealed that alone was lonely.
It was revealed that your smaller stature was a stronger base.
I learned that your strength covered my biggest weaknesses.
Me being here first meant nothing; you were specifically created because I needed help.
I could not love alone.
Loving only myself became lonely.
I was good, but you made me great.
Loving you became a goal.
Loving you became an action that made me feel good.

Loving you specifically, because I could not start new love with an old way. You were specific, you were different, you were what I have never experienced; bringing in a failed experience wouldn't result in our future success. I was tired of failing to love the way you needed because I valued my routine.

I admit that what I was used to was not going to work this time.

I had to adjust.

You deserved my growth.

You deserved my specificity.

Because I realized that you were created "specifically" for me.

Why abuse what was "specifically" made for me?

My "ready" changed when I met you. My "ready" changed because I wanted you. My "ready" changed when I matured enough to be specific. My "ready" changed when we met. My "ready" changed when I realized I didn't want to lose another great thing.

I wanted to do whatever was necessary for you to be with me. I wanted to do what was necessary for me to be with you. What I wanted prompted me to do what I needed.

I needed to be specific, throw out the game-plan, and change my focus. I became attentive to what was in front of me as opposed to avoiding what I had been through.

Specifically loving you.

PERSPECTIVE

Sometimes we approach and practice routine with the people we meet and we miss the opportunity to really know the person and ourselves in relationship with that person. Getting away from the constructs of our plan helps us really address our needs and wants with the person we engage with. We sometimes date from a deficit where we are looking to date what we didn't have in our last relationship. We target one thing and miss so many other things. We fail to ask questions because we think we know how to specifically love someone with our general tactics. Ask yourself, where did the design of your plan come from? Who told you how to love a stranger? What rules supersede the importance of getting to know the person specifically so you can learn to like, love, and build with the person as opposed to your plan?

TAKE IT PERSONAL

_____

_____

_____

_____

_____

_____

_____

Dear Future Wife

Chapter 33

DEAR FUTURE WIFE: WITHOUT GUILT

I want to be honest.
I can't wait until we say "I do".
I feel bottled up inside and I am ready to release everything I was designed to do.
Designed to please you.
Designed to protect you.
Designed to make sure you are satisfied.
Designed to make sure you are always okay and when you aren't, I am designed to put in that work to bring you to a better place.
I get in moods that I know are made for a marriage.
I misused them in the past and left myself less than, others greater than, and "us" struggling to find equality.
Those moods are for show but can be somewhat described as:
A mood to look at you and tell you I love you through my eyes.
Tell you I miss you through my lips.
Tell you I want you by a deep breath.
Tell you I will protect you by my hug.
My smile will be your sigh of relief.
My holding of your hand is me guiding you.
Not feeling guilty about possibly holding the wrong hand.
Not feeling guilty for mishandling your trust.
Not feeling guilty… because the connection of our mind, body, and soul will remain forever.

Not feeling guilty about staring at you while you dress.

Not feeling guilty for touching you inappropriately because you are mine and I am yours.

Not feeling guilty for kissing you with enough passion to make you forget all of the bad times.

Not feeling guilty for giving you my heart to hold, my mind to influence, and my soul to pray for genuinely.

I say genuinely because some pray for you with contingencies.

They will tell you they want you to succeed and do things behind your back that will cause you to bleed.

I want to pray for each other.

Not pray for each other to meet each other's wants.

But pray for each other's well-being, trusting that will include us in each other's happiness.

I don't want the guilt of performing marital duties during single living.

I don't want the guilt of disappointing someone because we don't meet each other's love.

I don't want the guilt of sharing my words with someone I am not married to…

Dear Future Wife, our marriage will not be "blah"…

Touching you without guilt.

Loving you without guilt.

PERSPECTIVE

There are times where we feel guilt, shame, disappointment, like we wasted efforts, or just out of sorts when it comes to dating and courting. We do things we regret. We tell ourselves we should be saving things for marriage. The truth is, we should be saving things for marriage. It's only difficult to shift to "preserving" because we already shared a lot. Allow yourself to practice self-forgiveness and separate the acts of the old from who you currently are. The difference between guilt and shame is guilt is what I did and shame is who I am. You are not the results of the experiences and decisions that you made. You are a person who can make different choices that align with where you want to be, how you want to be, what the relationship you desire and who you want to be with. There is relief and freedom in knowing the person you are married to is aligned with forever. How can you practice forgiveness? What would it look like to love without guilt?

TAKE IT PERSONAL

_____

_____

_____

_____

_____

_____

_____

DEAR FUTURE WIFE

Chapter 34

DEAR FUTURE WIFE: NO EXCUSE

I created love where it didn't exist. My concept of a relationship derived from a desire. The examples of catering spawned from the dream of receiving. The teaching of care revealed itself by guessing the results of how you want to feel.

The effort to please appeared internally from needing to fill a void I had growing up. I didn't see magic so I worked to uncover the mystery. What I saw were forgiveness gifts that were just enough. From that, I built a fairytale destined for truth. Reality doesn't save, it reveals. I decided to example. I decided to be what escaped me. Instead of teaching I focused on being studious. So many of us are teaching women how to be, how to learn what a man wants, how to please. So many are endorsing the message of what a woman needs to do and often times we are teaching women how to completely pursue and keep an incomplete man. I don't want to be that incomplete man keeping you guessing.

I focused on my part. I pray you are focusing on yours. I am not going to tell you what to do because this is about me. I'm not letting the lack of having an example keep me ignorant of what is right. I've seen a flower exchange before and my imagination created a scenario where a bouquet was handed to you with purpose. My idea of love may seem unrealistic, but my effort to achieve the creation of the environment that escaped me, won't be. I heard of food being ordered/delivered and I imagined me looking up your favorite dish online and recreating it with my own culinary effort. The effort to cook it myself and have it ready when you get home. Preparing it while you're resting with your feet up. I am not taking away from the delivery system; sometimes I just want to be the deliverer.

I am creating an environment that once was invisible to me. Caring without a "but," endorsing communication without attacks. Having safety in building. Not comparing, because that led to previous destruction. No more excuses of not witnessing love in action. No more excuses of "I wasn't raised that way." No more excuses of little-to-no-teaching. No more excuses of failure derailing me. No more excuses of playing it safe.

Creating love where it wants and needs to exist. Relationship concept desired is revealed in reality. Receiving matched my giving, emulating the effort to sustain. Revelation came from the guess, trial and error, and genuine effort to fight past the excuses.

No more excuses! Let's go walk on water together!

PERSPECTIVE

Think of how many times we as men have said to ourselves, "I didn't have an example." This may be due to our fathers not being there, our fathers being there but not being good husbands because their fathers didn't show them how to be a husband. The men in our community aren't showing us faithfulness. Society has pushed unhealthy thoughts and practices of what a man is supposed to look like and how to operate. We have to stop allowing the lack of knowledge or experience stop us from learning how to be a good boyfriend, fiance' and husband. We have taken so much time to learn so many things and this is another one to learn through studying, humility, openness, prayer, partnerships and support. What does your circle look like? Who are you hanging out with? Who and what influences your sense of self? What does vulnerability look like in learning how to be a better man, partner, husband?

TAKE IT PERSONAL

_____

_____

_____

_____

_____

_____

DEAR FUTURE WIFE

Chapter 35

DEAR FUTURE WIFE: YOU'RE WORTH THE WORK

I'm distracted by the thoughts of you.

Although, I'm sometimes overwhelmed with all the work I have to do.

I know you are worth every speck of blood, sweat, and tear.

I faced and erased everything that a man with pride would fear.

I pause to think of the times of us two.

How immaculately God matched your eyes to your smile to your heart, I have no clue.

All I know is that it took me years to learn how to be the man you needed me to be.

I wasn't always patient but the wait was for what I am now able to see.

Me for you and you for me.

The thought of you sends a chill throughout my entire being.

This is what people have been describing, this is what they have been meaning.

I'm excited by the thought of you, plus me equals us.

I'm excited that we made a decision to move past our past and purposely trust.

The prayer began with preparation for me to become what I needed to be, in order to be what you want.

What you want is a man with broad shoulders and a strong frame to carry your burdens when they are too much to bare alone.

A man that puts you on his shoulders to help you see over your insecurities.

A man who will stop what he is doing to just listen.
A man who will wipe your tears with kisses and remind you of reasons to smile.
A man who will grab your hand when it's time to pray.
A man that sees your beauty without looking at you and makes you feel beautiful when you feel you are at your ugliest moments.
I realized in order to get you to "fall" in love with me, I would have to stand firm on the things that are needed to get you there.
I have to work love and love to work.
Once we get there, I will not stop doing the things I did.
They will manifest differently so that you won't get used to my love.

PERSPECTIVE

Relationships require work and the sacrifices we make are worth the results of a healthy relationship. A healthy relationship doesn't mean a perfect relationship, it means to be committed to the relationship even when the person disappoints you. There are times where you make not like your partner and you have to still contribute to their happiness. This is where ego is put to the side and you choose they are still worth the effort. Once you work on yourself and know your worth, the woman or man you meet will match the efforts you put in yourself. Giving and taking will become less daunting and you won't be keeping score to measure the worth of your effort. The work won't be effortless; it will be pleasantly essential. How do you determine the worth of your efforts to love and have a relationship? What scores are you keeping that keeps you connected or pushes you to disconnect from someone? How much work have you done on yourself to be whole and to be matched and complemented?

TAKE IT PERSONAL

_____

_____

_____

_____

_____

_____

_____

Dear Future Wife

Chapter 36

MY VOW

You are God's timing. You are God's answer. You are God's response to any of my questions of who is she, where is she, and how will she be? You are the results of faith, prayers, and practice. Since I met you, my life has changed. Your words, your smile, your heart, your voice and your presence have elevated my soul. I vow to continue to learn you, unlearn parts of me, while relearning how to love. I was born to excel in all things and I finally get to excel in all things God has called a husband to be. Although we will have tons of fun, loving you will be no laughing matter. I'm not promising perfection but I vow to always stay connected and remember that God made you for me. Honoring you is honoring God! The past is the past, the future will be what it will be. Always know for sure, I will be present for you and me! Thank you for helping Nicholas see me as a husband!

Take it personal:
What are your vows to yourself?

CONNECT WITH BASHEA WILLIAMS

Twitter @BasheaWilliams

IG @BasheaWilliams

BasheaWilliams.com

ABOUT THE AUTHOR

Paul Bashea (Bah-Shay) Williams, LCSW-C, LICSW is a dedicated father, a Licensed Clinical Social Worker, Relationship Advisor, Entrepreneur and Author of the book Dear Future Wife: A man's guide and a woman's reference to healthy relationships. An entrepreneur who owns and operates his own private practice at Hearts In Mind Counseling where he works with vulnerable youth and specializes in marriage and family, couples, and individual counseling. His writing, acting, and public speaking has been featured in and on HBO, Men's Health Magazine, Essence Magazine, BET, Bustle, Roland Martin Show, Huffington Post, TV One, Radio One, TV Guide, national syndicated radio shows, ABC, NBC, FOX, CBS, movies, and conferences all over the nation.

Paul Bashea Williams attended East Tennessee State University in Johnson City, Tennessee for both his undergrad and graduate studies in Social Work. Since graduating he serves in various agencies as a Social Worker in hospital settings, community based wrap around services, independent living programs for youth, alternative school based therapeutic services, a government child welfare agency, and outpatient therapy settings until he opened up his own private practice which has been in operation since 2017. While running a private practice, Paul Bashea Williams has traveled the world speaking about the importance of your mental health.

Paul Bashea Williams has provided valuable insight on mental health, relationships, motivation, and parenting on a variety of panels and conferences. He is highly recruited and his work is valued as measurable and complete. He has years of providing counseling services for singles, couples, youth, families, groups and corporate entities. His goal is to influence healthy relationships by having comprehension, compromise, consideration, and an understanding of how people interact with one another. You can follow his work at BasheaWilliams.com, BasheaWilliams on Instagram, Facebook, and YouTube. His counseling services can be found at www.HeartsInMindCounseling.com